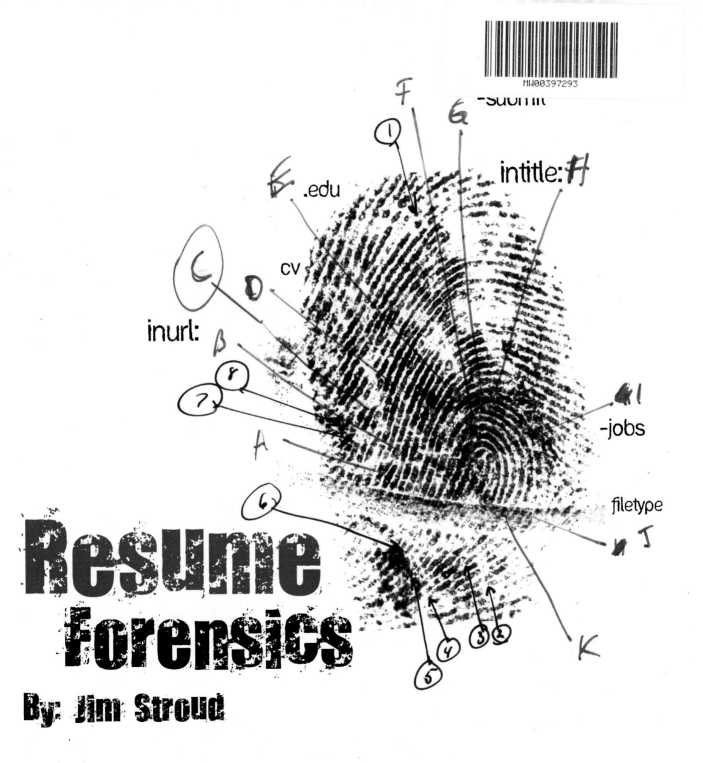

Resume Forensics

By: Jim Stroud

RESUME FORENSICS

By: Jim Stroud

Photo credits:

Cover: Vince Alongi / pg. 5: FutUndBeidl / pg 7: David Davies / pg. 18: H.Koppdelaney / pg. 91: Marc Smith

—THANK YOU—

Thank you to everyone and anyone who said **"good job,"** or shared one of my videos, listened to one of my podcasts, admired a photo I took, or laughed at one of my jokes, or commented on one of my blog posts, or retweeted me, gave me a plus one, or a Facebook "like." I heard you. I appreciate what you did. Thank you for encouraging me.

—Jim Stroud —

Thanks for being a friend!

HI!

IN THIS BOOK:

How to Search Google for free resumes and passive candidates. (I also share a few other resources while I'm at it. Good times!)

WHY WRITE IT THIS WAY?

I hope this book helps you meet all of your sourcing goals. My approach in writing this book is to write as little as possible. (Crazy, right?) People have short attention spans anyway so, squirrel...

ABOUT THE AUTHOR: linkedin.com/in/jimstroud

;)

If **you** can identify with this picture, this book is for you.

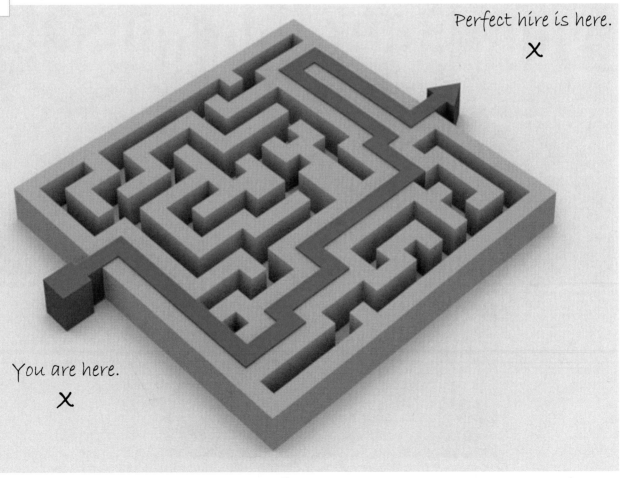

Perfect hire is here.
X

You are here.
X

Get ready to flex your sourcing muscles

Not actual size

PRESEARCH

1

SCENARIO: Hiring Manager wants you to find some talent for a specific requisition. Ideally, your meeting with them to discuss their request will happen **after** you have done the following.

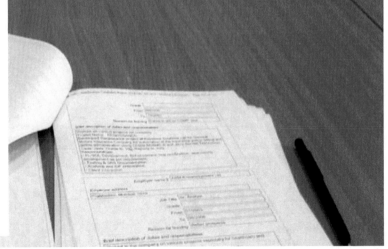

Analyze resumes in your ATS:

- Who was interviewed previously for the role?
- Where did they come from?
- Why were they turned down?
- If they were merely outshined, will the manager reconsider them?

Interview a co-worker in the role:

- What do they do everyday?
- What helps them to be successful on their job? (skills, knowledge)
- What are tools they use everyday?
- The people who work alongside them, what do they do?
- What are typical problems they deal with on the job?
- What did they do before working at your company?
- What personality traits would be helpful to excel on their job?

Google™

related:sprint.com

Web   Images   Maps   Shopping   More ▾   Search tools

About 184 results (0.16 seconds)

T-Mobile: Cell Phones | 4G Phones | iPhone and Android Phones
www.t-mobile.com/
Discover T-Mobile's best cell phones and plans with no annual contract including the iPhone and Android cell phones. Find affordable cell phones and flexible ...

Cell Phones - Smartphones: Cell Phone Service, Accessories ...
www.verizonwireless.com/
Discover the latest Cell Phones, Smartphones, Prepaid Devices, Tablets, Cell Phone Plans and Accessories from Verizon Wireless. The nation's largest 4G LTE ...

Sprint:
www.nextel.com/

AT&T Cell Phones, U-verse, Digital TV, DSL Internet, and Phone ...
www.att.com/
AT&T is a leader in telecommunication services, including cell phones, wireless, U-verse, digital TV, high speed internet, DSL, home phone, and bundled ...

MetroPCS

tropcs.com/
 provides No Contract Cell Phones and Low-Rate Prepaid Plans with

I'll get more into this later when I focus on Google specific search commands. For now, suffice to say, I am asking Google to find companies that are related to Sprint. As such, these would be competitor companies and/or companies operating in their space. For example: T-Mobile, Verizon, ATT and MetroPCS.

Web   Images   Maps   Shopping   More ▾   Search tools

Page 2 of about 193,000 results (0.14 seconds)

In the search string above, I am asking Google to fill in the blank for my search. This is the function of the asterix in Google searches. As a result, Google is finding search results that fit the pattern of what I am looking for. As you can see in the search results below, the following companies compete with Sprint: Clearwire, VoiceStream and Leap.

Sprint, Clearwire reach deal on wholesale pricing | Signal Strength ...
news.cnet.com › News › Signal Strength

 by Maggie Reardon - in 335 Google+ circles - More by Maggie Reardon
Apr 19, 2011 – And unlike **Clearwire, which also competes with Sprint** by selling a commercial 4G service directly to consumers, LightSquared will only sell ...

Omnipoint soars on VoiceStream merger - CNET News
news.cnet.com/Omnipoint-soars-on.../2100-12_3-258812.html
Jun 24, 1999 – **VoiceStream competes with Sprint** Corp (NYSE: FON), Vodafone Group Plc. (NYSE: VOD) and Airtouch Communications Inc. (NYSE: ATI).

[PDF] Leap Results Disappoint, Plans Improvement - Roe Equity Resea...
docs.roeequityresearch.com/press/08_03_10.pdf
File Format: PDF/Adobe Acrobat - Quick View
Aug 3, 2010 – **Leap also competes with Sprint**-Nextel unit Boost Mobile and America Movil's (AMXL.MX: Quote, Profile, Research, Stock. Buzz) (AMX.N: Quote ...

verizon patent litigation

Hmm... If companies are in court over patents, they obviously have similar tech.

TiVo settles **patent lawsuit** with **Verizon** for at least $250 million, is ...
www.engadget.com/.../tivo-settles-**patent-lawsuit**-with-**veriz**...

 by Richard Lawler - in 1,419 Google+ circles - More by Richard Lawler
Sep 24, 2012 – While some **patent** lawsuits continue to drag on, the battle
between TiVo and **Verizon** over DVR technology has come to a resolution.

Verizon To Pay TiVo $250M To Settle **Patent Lawsuit** | Cable ...
www.multichannel.com/news.../**verizon**-pay...**patent-lawsuit**/139417
Sep 24, 2012 – **Verizon** Communications will pay TiVo at least $250 million to settle the
DVR company's pending **patent litigation**, and the companies are also ...

allintitle: "Dell and * partner"

This search will find news or discussions where Dell has partnered with other companies.

Dell and Microsoft partner to deliver "open" turn-key cloud solutions ...
commweb-ps3.us.dell.com › Blogs › Enterprise › Inside Enterprise IT
Nov 6, 2010 – **Dell and Microsoft partner** to deliver "open" turn-key cloud solutions.
Dell.com » Community » Blogs » Enterprise » Inside Enterprise IT » **Dell** ...

Desktop Virtualization Just Got Simpler – **Dell and Citrix Partner** for ...
blogs.citrix.com/.../desktop-virtualization-just-got-simpler-dell-and-ci...
Mar 10, 2011 – Desktop Virtualization Just Got Simpler – **Dell and Citrix Partner** for an
End-to-End Desktop Virtualization Solution. By Natalie Lambert ...

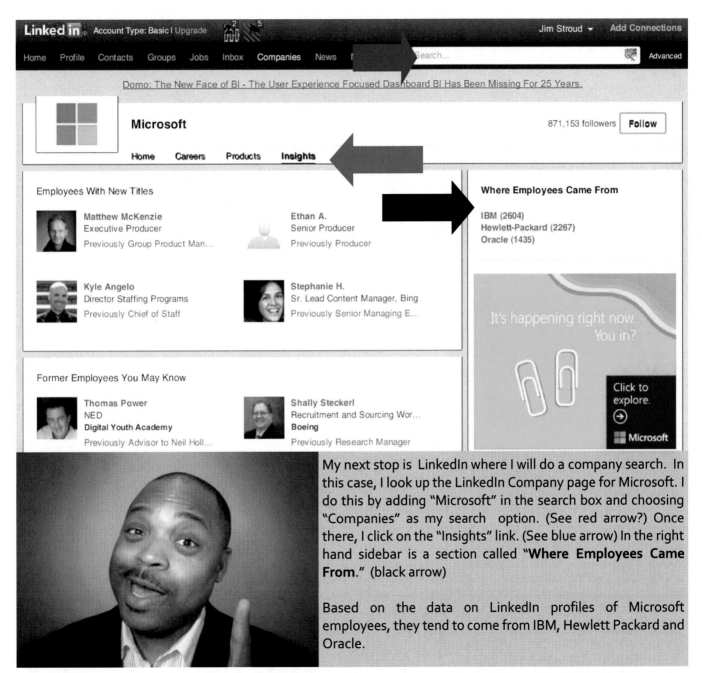

My next stop is LinkedIn where I will do a company search. In this case, I look up the LinkedIn Company page for Microsoft. I do this by adding "Microsoft" in the search box and choosing "Companies" as my search option. (See red arrow?) Once there, I click on the "Insights" link. (See blue arrow) In the right hand sidebar is a section called "**Where Employees Came From**." (black arrow)

Based on the data on LinkedIn profiles of Microsoft employees, they tend to come from IBM, Hewlett Packard and Oracle.

Incidentally, on this LinkedIn company page I can also see what are the most popular skills of Microsoft employees and which Microsoft employees are the most recommended. Good info to know.

LINKEDIN SKILLS   www.linkedin.com/skills

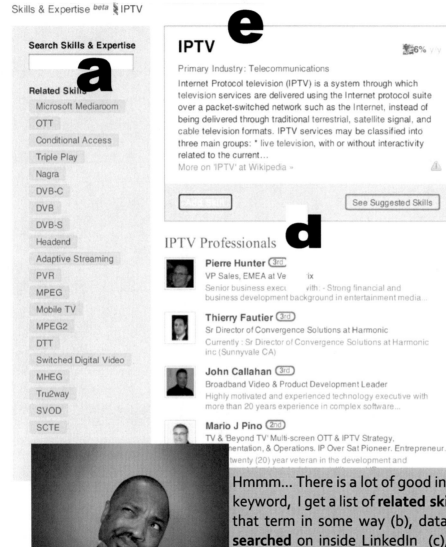

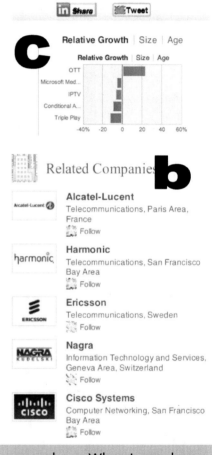

Skills & Expertise *beta* IPTV

Search Skills & Expertise

a

Related Skills
- Microsoft Mediaroom
- OTT
- Conditional Access
- Triple Play
- Nagra
- DVB-C
- DVB
- DVB-S
- Headend
- Adaptive Streaming
- PVR
- MPEG
- Mobile TV
- MPEG2
- DTT
- Switched Digital Video
- MHEG
- Tru2way
- SVOD
- SCTE

e

IPTV   6%

Primary Industry: Telecommunications

Internet Protocol television (IPTV) is a system through which television services are delivered using the Internet protocol suite over a packet-switched network such as the Internet, instead of being delivered through traditional terrestrial, satellite signal, and cable television formats. IPTV services may be classified into three main groups: * live television, with or without interactivity related to the current…

More on 'IPTV' at Wikipedia »

[Add Skill]   [See Suggested Skills]

d

IPTV Professionals

Pierre Hunter (3rd)
VP Sales, EMEA at Ve...ix
Senior business exec...with: - Strong financial and business development background in entertainment media...

Thierry Fautier (3rd)
Sr Director of Convergence Solutions at Harmonic
Currently : Sr Director of Convergence Solutions at Harmonic inc (Sunnyvale CA)

John Callahan (3rd)
Broadband Video & Product Development Leader
Highly motivated and experienced technology executive with more than 20 years experience in complex software...

Mario J Pino (2nd)
TV & 'Beyond TV' Multi-screen OTT & IPTV Strategy, ...nentation, & Operations. IP Over Sat Pioneer. Entrepreneur. ...twenty (20) year veteran in the development and

c

Relative Growth | Size | Age

Relative Growth | Size | Age
- OTT
- Microsoft Med...
- IPTV
- Conditional A...
- Triple Play

-40% -20 0 20 40 60%

Related Companies b

Alcatel-Lucent
Telecommunications, Paris Area, France
Follow

Harmonic
Telecommunications, San Francisco Bay Area
Follow

Ericsson
Telecommunications, Sweden
Follow

Nagra
Information Technology and Services, Geneva Area, Switzerland
Follow

Cisco Systems
Computer Networking, San Francisco Bay Area
Follow

Hmmm... There is a lot of good info I can use here. When I search on a keyword, I get a list of **related skills** (a), companies that are related to that term in some way (b), data on how often that term has been **searched** on inside LinkedIn (c), a list of people who feature this **keyword on their profiles** (d) and a **definition** of the keyword (e). If you were to scroll down this same page, there would be even more great data. (See following page)

12

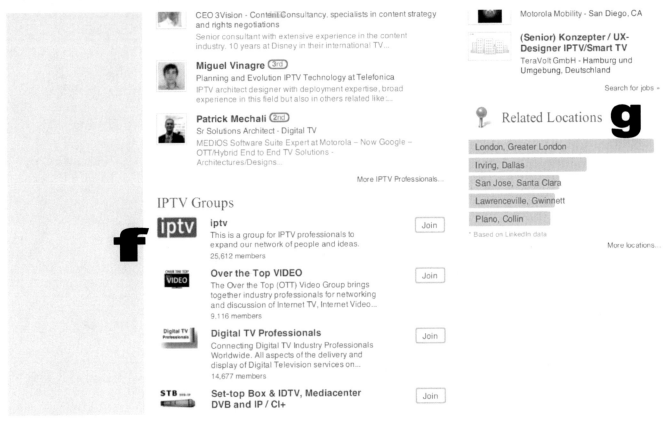

CEO 3Vision - Content Consultancy, specialists in content strategy and rights negotiations

Senior consultant with extensive experience in the content industry. 10 years at Disney in their international TV...

Miguel Vinagre (3rd)

Planning and Evolution IPTV Technology at Telefonica

IPTV architect designer with deployment expertise, broad experience in this field but also in others related like:...

Patrick Mechali (2nd)

Sr Solutions Architect - Digital TV

MEDIOS Software Suite Expert at Motorola – Now Google – OTT/Hybrid End to End TV Solutions - Architectures/Designs...

More IPTV Professionals...

IPTV Groups

iptv
This is a group for IPTV professionals to expand our network of people and ideas.
25,612 members
[Join]

Over the Top VIDEO
The Over the Top (OTT) Video Group brings together industry professionals for networking and discussion of Internet TV, Internet Video...
9,116 members
[Join]

Digital TV Professionals
Connecting Digital TV Industry Professionals Worldwide. All aspects of the delivery and display of Digital Television services on...
14,677 members
[Join]

Set-top Box & IDTV, Mediacenter DVB and IP / CI+
[Join]

Motorola Mobility - San Diego, CA

(Senior) Konzepter / UX-Designer IPTV/Smart TV
TeraVolt GmbH - Hamburg und Umgebung, Deutschland

Search for jobs »

Related Locations   g

London, Greater London

Irving, Dallas

San Jose, Santa Clara

Lawrenceville, Gwinnett

Plano, Collin

* Based on LinkedIn data

More locations...

LinkedIn is kind enough to give me a list of **LinkedIn Groups** dedicated to the keyword I am researching (f) and a list of **locations** (g). How does that work? To my knowledge, people who have the keyword I am searching for (in this case, IPTV) on their profile, tend to live in London, Dallas, Lawrenceville (GA), San Jose (CA) and so on.

Can you believe all this data is free? Thanks LinkedIn!

Careers

Search Again   Apply Online   Tell A Friend

Digital Project Manager

Job Code: SPM/ND   Location: Atlanta, GA

Bernard Hodes Group, part of Omnicom Group Inc. (NYSE: OMC), is the nation's leading recruitment communications company. We are seeking a highly motivated and organized individual for the position of Digital Project Manager to join our busy and dynamic National Digital Team. This position can be filled in either our New York or Atlanta offices.

In this challenging position, you will implement and manage innovative digital development projects that exceed client expectations.

The successful candidate will be a strategic and analytic thinker that can lead execution of web development, social, CRM, and mobile projects. Additionally, they will be extremely passionate about digital and will be able to inspire excellence across cross-functional teams.

Responsibilities:

ill exceed the client's goals.

dget and meets all stated goals in the project plan.

innovation, social, SEO, analytics, mobile, user

After all of the previous research has been done, I take a good look at the job description. (Go figure.)

- What are the keywords and phrases from the job description that will likely be on a candidate's resume?
- How does your competition title similar jobs? For example, is a Digital Strategist at your company the same thing as a Social Media Strategist somewhere else?
- Take out a thesaurus and research synonyms. "Troubleshoot" may be in the job description but, "make repairs" is on the resume." Make sense?
- What tools are listed in the job description? Make a list of competing tools. (see next page for an example of how to search for that).

If you have Google Suggest enabled in your Google Search preferences (and since it is the default, chances are you do), Google autocompletes your searches. Such being the case, to find a tool or product that competes with another, simply search: "product name vs" and Google will list rival products. Check out the examples below for clarification on what I mean.

java vs **javascript**

java vs **c++**

java vs **python**

java vs **.net**

asp vs **php**

asp vs **asp.net**

asp vs **saas**

asp vs **.net**

python vs

python vs **ruby**

python vs **php**

python vs **perl**

python vs **java**

 After doing **all** of the previous research, you should be more than prepared when meeting with the hiring manager about the role. Below are a few examples of how I imagine your chat may progress.

A) My research tells me that candidates we have interviewed in the past come from Company A and Company B. Companies X and Y are similar to Companies A & B. Such being the case, are you open to candidates from Companies X and Y and others similar to them?

B) I have noticed that Company G and Company V has tech that is similar to ours. Do you want to see candidates from these companies?

C) My research tells me that these types of candidates tend to live in Atlanta, Chicago and New York. Is relocation an option for the right candidate?

D) Would you consider candidates with alternative skills? For example, software Q competes with software X in the marketplace. If I present candidates skilled in software X instead of Q, would you be open to speaking with them?

Now I'm ready to speak with the hiring manager.

E) If I presented you with a list of related skills that I think may help me in finding candidates for you, would you review it to see if I am on target?

F) I have noticed that our competitor has a job called (insert job title here) that is very similar in scope to our job (insert job title here). Such being the case, shall I assume that you are open to viewing (competitor job title) resumes as well?

G) Whenever possible, I will give preference to those candidates that meet certain personality criteria. My research tells me that people who are quick learners and have an eye for detail will excel in this role. Is this your assertion as well?

H) My research tells me that before someone takes on this job title, they are either job title one, job title two or job title three. If I found someone with enough relevant experience in those roles, would you consider them?

I) I think you have it from here.

;-)

OMG

This is a lot of work!

If this seems like a lot of work that's because it is a lot of work. However, it is SO worth it. It will save you time by helping you present quality candidates verses a deluge of resumes. Make sense?

Plus, Hiring Managers will appreciate you more.

Tip:
Keep research on all the jobs you source for. This will make it easier for other recruiters sourcing for similar jobs.

2

In this section, I will focus on search methods that will work on Google, Yahoo and Bing. I will also touch on being efficient.

Google™

YAHOO!®

bing™

I love me some Google. However, it is necessary to search multiple search engines because there is **less than 1% overlap** in search engine results.

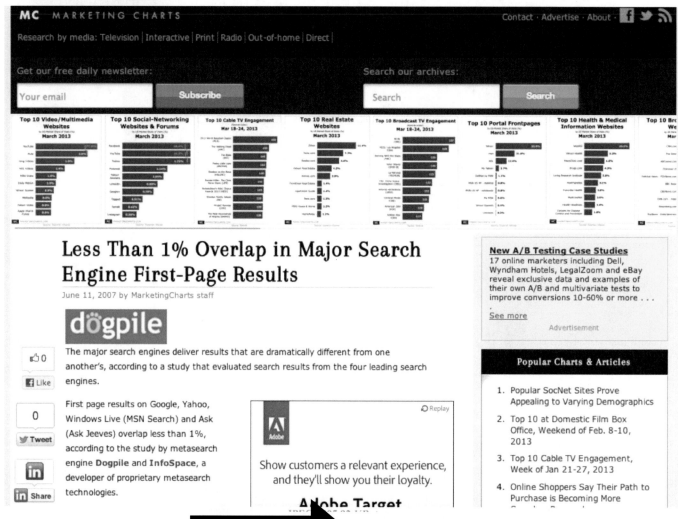

See for yourself!

Universal Syntax

All search engines are **not** the same. However in some instances, there is a shared language.

inurl: searches for a keyword in the URL of a web document.

intitle: Searches for a keyword in the title of a web document.

site: Restricts search results to a particular domain.

filetype: Restricts results to a particular format. (i.e. PDF, DOCX)

 - The minus sign restricts a keyword of phrase from your results.

" " Quotes asks the search engine to find an exact phrase.

These commands work on Google, Yahoo and Bing.

site:lockheedmartin.com "principal engineer"

Web   Images   Maps   Shopping   More ▾   Search tools

About 23 results (0.19 seconds)

Lockheed Martin · Search
www.lockheedmartin.com/us/search.html?q=engineer&start=70
Results 71 - 80 of 250 – Robert Szczerba, TEAM **principal engineer** at Lockheed
Martin Systems Integratic███████████. Our 'mission-centric' approach will ...

[PDF] 2011 Groundwater Monitoring Report February ... - Lockheed Martin
www.lockheedmartin.com/content/dam/.../text-2011-gwmr.PDF
File Format: PDF/Adobe Acrobat - Quick View
Feb 17, 2012 – Lockheed Martin Tallevast Site. Katherine L. Thalman, P.G.. Senior
Geologist. Gary Wroblewski. **Principal Engineer**. Guy Kaminski, P.E. ...

[PDF] 2011 Annual Groundwater Collection ... - Lockheed Martin
www.lockheedmartin.com/.../...
File Format: PDF/Adobe Acrobat
Mar 29, 2012 – **Principal Engineer**/Engineer of Record. NY PE License #074527-1.
Prepared for: Lockheed Martin Corporation. Prepared by: ARCADIS of New ...

Lockheed Martin · pr_mission_LockheedMartinHonorsSixOw
www.lockheedmartin.com/us/.../LockheedMartinHonorsSixOw.html
Mar 5, 2009 – Steve Moraites is a **principal engineer** and expert in system engineering
particularly with█████████ivability and sensor design. He has ...

[PDF] 2010 Groundwater Monitoring Report Lockheed Martin Tallevast ...

In this example, I am asking Google to search the Lockheed Martin website for mentions of the phrase "Principal Engineer." Among the results : Robert Szczerba, Gary Wroblewski and Steve Moraites.

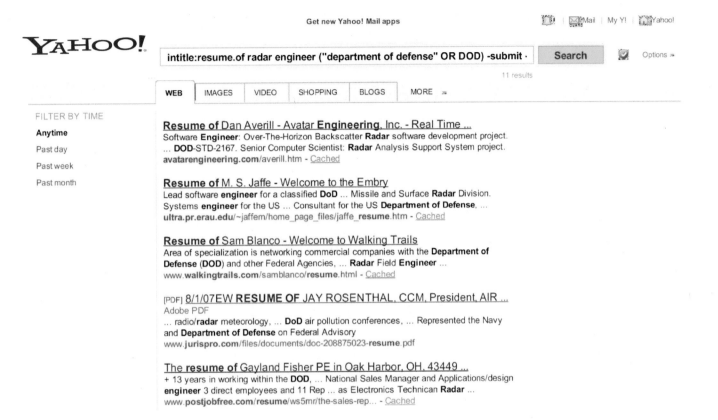

In this example, I am looking for a radar engineer with DOD experience. I do not want the words "submit," "apply," "your," "sample" or "example" in my results as they typically would be on job descriptions. I also have added a period between the words "resume" and "of." I very well could have searched and received the same results if I searched this way: intitle:"resume of" radar engineer ("department of defense" OR DOD) -submit -apply -your -sample -example intitle:resume missile education engineering -submit -apply -your -sample -example

In this example, I am looking for an engineer with a background in missiles. I could go on ad nauseum with these search examples. (Ooh, aren't I fancy?) But, I think you get the picture. Now, let me show you something really cool that pushes my point about using more than one search engine even further.

A metasearch engine is a search engine that searches search engines and Dogpile.com is one. Specifically, it searches Google, Yahoo and Yandex. In the example below I am searching for the phrase "natural language processing" on resumes that are cited on college websites.

My search → intitle:resume site:edu "natural language processing"

In the search results of Dogpile.com we see that some results are exclusive to certain search engines whereas others are shared. **Search result A** could only be found on Yahoo.

Resume for Matthias Ruhl
people.csail.mit.edu/ruhl/resume.html • Found exclusively on: Google
Computer Science: Cryptography and Cryptanalysis, Programming **Languages**, Topics in Theoretical Computer Science, **Natural Language Processing**, ...

Processing - definition of **Processing** by the Free Online ...
www.thefreedictionary.com/**processing** • Found exclusively on: Yahoo! Search
proc·ess 1 (pr s s, pr s s) n. pl. proc·ess A series of actions, changes, or functions bringing about a result: the ...

A

Resume (PD US) - Graduate Computer Science Systems
paul.rutgers.edu/~zhipeng/Vision.Zhipeng.Zhao.doc • Found exclusively on: Google
document retrieval, **natural language processing**. Department of Computer Science, Rutgers University: 2003-2009. Research assistant under the supervision of ...

Language Reference (API) \ **Processing** 2+
www.**processing**.org/reference/ • Found exclusively on: Yahoo! Search
Processing is an electronic sketchbook for developing ideas. It is a context for learning fundamentals of computer programming within the context of the ...

Professional Resume - Computer Science - University of ...
www.cs.umass.edu/~yhkim/yhkim_cv.pdf • Found exclusively on: Google
Research Interest Information Retrieval, Text anguage rocessing. Education. ▫ University of Massachusetts Amherst, USA ...

B

Noriko Tomuro's Resume - DePaul University
condor.depaul.edu/ntomuro/cv/cv.html • Found exclusively on: Yahoo! Search

Search result A is exclusive to **Yahoo. Search result B** is exclusive to **Google**. Just in case you missed it, I have underlined the language in red where it says, "Found exclusively on...."

Although I did not scan beyond the first couple of pages of results, chances are that I would find search results that are exclusive to Yandex as well. And for those who don't know, **Yandex** is a search engine based in Russia. Its very popular in certain circles. Hah! I can just imagine the look on some of your faces. Actually, I am mimicking that gaze on the next page.

 Let me share with you search commands that are exclusive to Google.

Google "I am a Software * Engineer"

Web   Images   Maps   Shopping   More ▾   Search tools

About 5,700,000 results (0.49 seconds)

QA, Test engineer's Payscale — Software Testing Help
www.softwaretestinghelp.com/qa-test-engineers-payscale/
by Vijay S - in 1,096 Google+ circles - More by Vijay S
I am a Software Test Engineer with over 3 years of experience in manaual and automation testing.My domain has been purely finance oriented.I am looking for a ...

I am a software test engineer with 3+ years experience in manual ...
kochi.olx.in › Jobs › Technology Jobs
SREENATH.G 'Gopasree' Manjeri-676121, Kerala, India E-mail: sreenumail@gmail.com Telephone:0483 2766781 Mobile: 91-9387201081 Career Vision: To ...

Software Dev | Be Your Future
www.beyourfuture.net/category/uk-intern/software-dev/
Mar 8, 2013 – Posted on September 14, 2012 by beyourfuture. Hey, I'm Chris and **I am a Software Development Engineer** working on Microsoft Mediaroom.

Jack Tesolin | LinkedIn
www.linkedin.com/in/jacktesolin
San Francisco Bay Area - Software Engineer in Test III at FactSet Research Systems Currently, **I am a Software Development Engineer** in Test, developing and maintaining API and unit tests using C# and the Visual Studio Unit Testing Framework ...

Google refers to the asterix as the "**wildcard**." The wildcard commands asks Google to fill in the blank. In the example above, notice how Google finds search results that fits where a missing word is. In one case, "test" and in another, "Development."

Google™   ~job   🎤

Web   Images   Maps   Shopping   More ▾   Search tools

About 10,250,000,000 results (0.29 seconds)

Careerbuilder.com: **Jobs** & **Job** Search Advice, **Employment** & **Care**...
www.**career**builder.com/
Looking for a new **job**? Get advice or search over 1.6 million **jobs** on the largest **job** site, set alerts to be first in line and have new **jobs** emailed to you.

Welcome to **Salary**.com - **Salary**.com
www.**salary**.com/
Skills management software for human capital management and to build skills inventories. Features company profile, and details of solutions.
Salary.com - Salary Range - Salary.com Salary Wizard - Mid Career

Job Search | one search. all **jobs**. Indeed.com
www.indeed.com/
Click here to find millions of **jobs** from thousands of company web sites, **job** boards and newspapers. one search. all **jobs**. Indeed.
Jobs - Find jobs - Salary Search - Job Trends
2,485 people +1'd this

Monster.com: Find **Jobs**. Build a Better **Career**. Find Your Calling.
www.monster.com/
Find the **job** that's right for you. Use Monster's resources to create a killer **resume**, search for **jobs**, prepare for interviews, and launch your **career**.

Job (biblical figure) - Wikipedia, the free encyclopedia
en.wikipedia.org/wiki/**Job**_(biblical_figure)

This is the **tilde**. When you add it in front of a keyword on Google, it looks for synonyms and/or similar words. In the example above, notice how certain words are bolded? Google thinks the words: career, employment, job and resume are related to the word "job."

intitle:resume 2006..2011-present education healthcare programmer ext:pdf

Web   Images   Maps   Shopping   More ▾   Search tools

About 3,520 results (0.26 seconds)

[PDF] **Resume** Samples - CCO - Purdue University
https://www.cco.purdue.edu/Student/**Resume**/**Resume**Samples.pdf
File Format: PDF/Adobe Acrobat - Quick View
August **2011-Present** ... Properly answered **medical** questions in person and on the
phone. Activities and ... **EDUCATION**: Purdue University, West Lafayette, IN. Bachelor
of ... MATLAB: **Programming** tool used to solve complex calculations ...

[PDF] Sample **Resume** - Profession Direction, LLC
www.professiondirection.net/success.../it-**resume**-sample.pdf
File Format: PDF/Adobe Acrobat
ADVANCED SUPPORT TECHNICIAN | DataWorks | Lansing, Michigan. **2007 –
Present**. Provide accurate technology solutions and **programming** for **healthcare** ...

[PDF] Werner Wothke, **Resume** - SmallWaters
www.smallwaters.com/werner/Werner%20Wothke,%20**Resume**.pdf
File Format: PDF/Adobe Acrobat - Quick View
More than 9 years experience in large-scale **educational** assessment and reporting; and
more than 12 ... Leading high-level creative teams of psychometricians, **programmers**,
research associates ... **2006-PRESENT**. Principal ... Provided statistical consulting
services to D & B **HealthCare** Information and university-based ...

numrange   The **numrange** commands is represented in the two dots. It allows you to search within a range of numbers. In the example above, I am looking for resumes that have 2006-present, 2007-present, 2008-present, 2009-present, 2010-present or 2011-present cited therein.

Google
related:prudential.com

Web   Images   Maps   Shopping   More ▾   Search tools

About 175 results (0.17 seconds)

New York Life
www.newyorklife.com/
Life Insurance, Annuities, Long-Term Care Insurance, and Mutual Funds from the
Company You Keep.

State Farm - Car Insurance Quotes - Save on Auto Insurance
www.statefarm.com/
State Farm offers more discounts to more drivers than any other insurance company.
Get free insurance quotes today and see how you can save on auto, home, ...

Auto Insurance Quotes - Car Insurance | Allstate Online Quote
www.allstate.com/
Get auto insurance quotes at Allstate.com. You're In Good Hands With Allstate. Allstate
also offers insurance for your home, motorcycle, RV, as well as financial ...

American International Group, Inc - Insurance from AIG in the US
www.aig.com/
International insurance and financial services organization, with operations in
approximately 130 countries and jurisdictions.

related

If you remember, I shared the **related** command earlier. This command looks for websites that are similar or related to a certain URL. In this case, websites that are akin to Prudential.com include StateFarm.com and AllState.com.

Google allintitle: resume of software developer ext:pdf

Web   Images   Maps   Shopping   More ▾   Search tools

5 results (0.24 seconds)

[PDF] **Resume of** Suzanne Berger **Software Developer** for Visual Effe…
resume.zanefx.com/**Resume**_SuzanneBerger.pdf
File Format: PDF/Adobe Acrobat - Quick View
Resume of Suzanne Berger. Software Developer for Visual Effects and Animation. Cell:
415-720-7414 Email: tangle1@mindspring.com Web: …

Resume of Suzanne Berger **Software Developer** for … - Pdf Ebooks
pdf.ebooks6.com/**Resume-of**-Suzanne-Berger-**Software-Developer**-f…
Resume of Suzanne Berger Software Developer for Visual Effects and Book: • Member
of Autodesk Developer Network (ADN). Professional Experience .

Resume of Suzanne Berger **Software Developer** for Visual Effects …
pdf.ebooks6.com/**Resume-of**-Suzanne-Berger-**Software-Developer**-f…
▓▓▓▓▓ Rating: 10/10 - 13 votes
Book Description: • Member of Autodesk Developer Network (ADN). Professional
Experience . Pipeline Developer – Walt Disney Imagineering (Superior), Los …

[PDF] **RESUME OF** PRABHJOT SINGH BAKSHI … - Elucit Software
…ftware.com/pdf/1301937159e.pdf

The **allintitle** command says that all the keywords must
appear in the title of the page. The **EXT** command I am
using is the same as "filetype." Notice how the search terms
are **not** touching the "allintitle" command? (Unlike how EXT is
being used.)

33

allintext: "cloud computing" present education georgia tech "references upo 🎤

Web · Images · Maps · Shopping · More ▾ · Search tools

About 57 results (0.16 seconds)

Marquis Walsh | LinkedIn
www.linkedin.com/in/marquiswalsh
Greater Boston Area - Instructional Designer at University of New Hampshire
Education. Syracuse University; Castleton State College. Connections ... **Present**:
Instructional Designer, University of New Hampshire ... http://www.
hannafordcareercenter.org/programs/arts-humanities/video-**tech**-arts/ ... CNN Headline
News, Atlanta, **Georgia**. http://www.cnn.com/HLN/ ... *Stories/**References upon
request**.

Marquis Walsh | LinkedIn
www.linkedin.com/pub/marquis-walsh/06/398/690
Greater Boston Area - Instructional Designer at University of New Hampshire
Location: Greater Boston Area; Industry: **Education** Management ... **Present**:
Instructional Designer, University of New Hampshire ... Video **Tech** Arts Instructor.
Patricia A. ... CNN Headline News, Atlanta, **Georgia**. http://www.cnn.com/HLN/ ... *
Stories/**References upon request**. ... Conversations On **Cloud Computing** logo ...

Careers at Meraki
https://www.meraki.com/jobs
... used the power of **cloud computing** to make truly plug and play large scale
networks. .... Brazil; **Georgia**; Canada; UK; Singapore; Illinois/ Wisconsin; New York
City; Detroit; South Korea ..... Must be able to provide **references upon request**. ...
providing technical **education** to customers and partners, building collateral and ...

[PDF] John O'Sullivan - Orange County Public Schools
ocps.net/sb/Documents/.../John%20O'Sullivan.pdf
PDF/Adobe Acrobat - Quick View

Ad

G...
ww
Sa
Ap

HF
ww
Re
Co

Cl
ww
Int
Fin
Int

Ce
ww
Clo
On
Am
foll

Ce
ww

allintext

With the "allintext" command, you are asking Google to insure that all of the query words must appear in the text of the page. (Part of the search in the screenshot is hidden. The missing part is "references upon request."). Notice how the search terms are not touching "allintext?"

Google   allinurl: resume of slideshare   🎤   [

Web   Images   Maps   Shopping   More ▾   Search tools

About 2,470 results (0.12 seconds)

Resume of accounts officer
www.**slideshare**.net/sayedajju/**resume-of**-accounts-officer-11845721
Mar 3, 2012 – Resume of accounts officer Document Transcript. Resume-Accounts
Officer Saturday, March 03, 2012 Sayed A.H. Rizvi Mobile-Qatar: ...

The Journey of Jairus [visual resume] - @empoweredpres
www.**slideshare**.net/.../the-journey-**of**-jairus-visual-**resume**-empowere...
Dec 10, 2012 – Get to know Jairus! One of our awesome interns here at Empowered
Presentations!

Resume of dhanashree
www.**slideshare**.net/.../**resume-of**-dhanashree-16176979
Jan 25, 2013 – Vidya Prasarak Mandal, Thane Dr. V. N. Bedekar Institute of
Management Studies (DR VN BRIMS)

Veteran Seo Analyst Resume Of Bhaskar Das
www.**slideshare**.net/.../veteran-seo-analyst-**resume-of**-bhaskar-das
Jan 25, 2013 – Endeavoring 3yrs in internet Market with enormous knowledge and skills.
Have vast experience in SEO,SMO & PPC. Find me Skype@ ...

Resume Of Dieter R. Hertling
hare.net/dieterhertling/**resume-of**-dieter-r-hertling
– Resume of Dieter R. Hertling - Learning and Development Executive,

The "allinurl" commands says all query words (in this case "resume of slideshare") must appear in the URL of a search result. Above, I am seeking resumes that are posted on the site Slideshare.net. Notice how the search terms are not touching "allinurl?"

 intext:hotmail.com intext:programming intext:expected.graduation.date ext:d

Web   Images   Maps   Shopping   More ▾   Search tools

About 71 results (0.21 seconds)

[DOC] <u>Sara Andersen - Texas A&M University</u>
https://parasol.tamu.edu/people/bs/.../481/.../lma_Aggie_Resumes.do...
File Format: Microsoft Word - Quick View
Expected Graduation date: December 2003. High School: Prout High School ... St. ¨
College Station, TX 77845. Phone: 979.xxx-xxxx ¨ e-mail: ita@**hotmail.com** ...

[DOC] <u>HAZEM ADEL RADY - Webs</u>
www.freewebs.com/hazemrady/HRCV.doc
File Format: Microsoft Word - Quick View
HAZEM ADEL RADY hazemrady@**hotmail.com** ... **Expected Graduation date**:
December 2005 ... PLC **Programming** (SIMATIC Manager V5.1, PLCSIM V5.0) ...

[DOC] <u>ELIZABETH E</u>
xa.yimg.com/kq/groups/.../Elizabeth+Walden+resume+(2009).doc
File Format: Microsoft Word - View as HTML
elizabethwalden@**hotmail.com** ... **Expected Graduation Date**: December 2009 ...
Assisted in orientation **programming** for first-year international students.

[DOC] <u>JOB HUNTING PACKET all pages</u>
https://myportal.bsd405.org/.../...
File Format: Microsoft Word - Quick View
Expected Graduation Date: June 2012. Related coursework: Accounting (2 years),
Business and Marketing, **Programming**, Computer Keyboarding, Calculus ...

intext

The "**intext**" command says that the terms must appear in the text of the page. (Searching without the "intext" command looks for words anywhere on the page.)

 **Google**™   link:https://developers.google.com   🎤

Web   Images   Maps   Shopping   More ▾   Search tools

About 310 results (0.15 seconds)

AngelHack Hackathon & Accelerator
angelhack.com/
AngelHack is the best damn hackathon you've ever seen, filled with gourmet meals, toys, shirts, shwag, massages, and the best prizes around like cash, tech ...

Google I/O 2013
https://developers.google.com/events/io/travel
Hotel Accommodations. All hotels are located within walking distance of Moscone West. Attendees are responsible for their own reservations and payment.

About Bret Taylor
backchannel.org/about
Bret Taylor About Me Feed. About Bret Taylor. I am currently working on a new startup in Silcon Valley with my friend Kevin Gibbs. I was most recently Chief ...

The Go Programming Language Blog: New Talk and Tutorials
blog.golang.org/2010/05/new-talk-and-tutorials.html
 by Andrew Gerrand - More by Andrew Gerrand
May 5, 2010 – Rob Pike recently gave a talk at Stanford's Computer Systems Colloquium (EE380). Titled "Another Go at Language Design", the presentation ...

Developer Advocates - Google Developer Relations Japan
sites.google.com/site/devreljp/developer-advocates - Translate this page
Eiji Kitamura (北村 英志) 北村 英志はGoogleのデベロッパーアドボケイトとして、Chrome Extension やChrome Web Store、HTML5 をはじめとしたフロントエンド技術

link

The "**link**" command (above) is being used to find pages that link to https://developers.google.com. **TIP**: Finding sites that interest developers is a way of finding developers. Just sayin'...

 **Google** allinanchor: useful java code [

Web   Images   Maps   Shopping   More ▾   Search tools

About 125,000,000 results (0.28 seconds)

20 very useful Java code snippets for Java Developers
viralpatel.net › Home › Java

 by Viral Patel - in 198 Google+ circles - More by Viral Patel
May 13, 2009 — 20 very useful Java code snippets for Java Developers. Java
Code Snippets. parse xml in java, string to date, generate json, current method
...

Useful Eclipse Java Code Templates - Stack Overflow
stackoverflow.com/questions/.../**useful**-eclipse-**java-code**-templates
30 answers
You can create various Java code templates in Eclipse via the ... Create Log4J logger:
${:import(org.apache.log4j.Logger)} private static final Logger _logger ...

Useful Java Code
fractalsoftworks.com › ... › Starsector › Modding › Modding Resources
13 posts - 7 authors - Aug 18, 2012
I thought it might be useful to have a thread that contains example code for commonly
needed mod features. Eventually I hope to have a long ...

Java Developer Most Useful Books | Java Code Geeks
www.javacodegeeks.com › Core Java
Jun 22, 2011 — There's a lot of consensus in the Java world about which books rise to
the top of the Must Read list. At the risk of pointing out the obvious, here's ...

allinanchor

REMINDER: Finding sites that interest developers is a way of finding
developers. In the above, I am using the "**allinanchor**" command to
find links that have **all** of the words "useful java code" in them.

Notice how the search terms are not touching "allinanchor?" Pretty
much search commands that begin with "allin" operate this way.

Google

(inanchor:gmail.com | inanchor:hotmail) "penetration tester" inanchor:resum

Web   Images   Maps   Shopping   More ▾   Search tools

1 result (0.17 seconds)

Sameh Sabry | Security Consultant – **Penetration Tester** – Ethical ...
samehsabry.wordpress.com/
Mar 22, 2013 – Security Consultant - **Penetration Tester** - Ethical Hacker - Technical Writer - Drummer - Cook.

inanchor	The **"inanchor"** command says that the terms must appear in the text of links on the page. (Above, notice the search words in the title.)

* Quick side note:
(keyword **|** keyword) is the same as searching (keyword OR keyword). The symbol I am using for "OR" in the screenshot is called the pipe command. Don't want to confuse you. ;-)

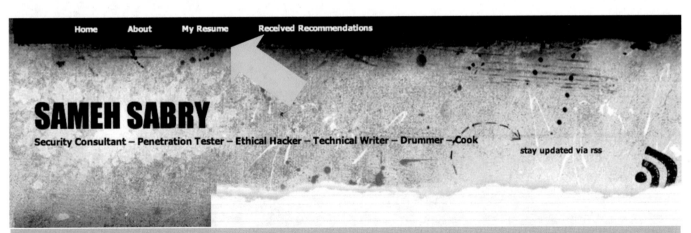

In the top image I am looking for a "penetration tester" on a page that has the keywords gmail or hotmail in a link. Also, the word "resume" is in a link as well. After the search, there was only one result. On that resulting page, there is a "my resume" link at the top (see arrow) and a link to a blog post about Hotmail (not shown above). Good, but I was hoping for an email address. Oh well.

WHOA!

Starting to feel information overload?

Well, that's the advantage of having this is in a book. You can always put it down and come back to it.

Well, just in case you do not have information overload (and even if you do), here is a list of keywords and phrases you can use to find free resumes on Google. They are basically, a list of words typical to resumes and job descriptions. Enjoy!

EXCLUDE: JOB DESCRIPTION KEYWORDS

Apply	careers	Benefits	recruiter
Request	reply	wizard	recruit
Templates	preferred	free	download
Template	example	your	tips
Jobs	submit	paste	hiring
Job	eoe	search	"looking for"
Post	"equal opportunity employer"	order	
Sample	send	openings	

INCLUDE: KEYWORDS ON RESUMES

Education	summary	objective	references	experience
Hobbies	personal	references	GPA	volunteer
Phone	email	certifications	internship	cv
Vitae	responsibilities	Awards/honors	academic	overview

INCLUDE: COMMON PHRASES ON RESUMES

"managing a staff"	"to gain employment"	"proven track record"
"my years"	"available upon request"	"Team player"
"extensive experience"	"expected graduation date"	"Problem Solver"
"a position that will allow me"	"in applying for this position"	"fast paced"
"I will be utilizing"	"results oriented"	Entrepreneurial
Dynamic	Highly motivated	Communication skills
"track record"	"problem solving"	analytical
Effective	specialized	detail oriented

INCLUDE: COMMON PHRASES ON RESUMES

"salary negotiable"   "Responsible for"   "Experience working in"   "self starter"
"hard working"   "performance oriented"   "committed to excellence"   "solutions oriented"
"Positive attitude"   "quick learner"   "work ethic"   "go to person"

"Track record of success"   "served as company spokesperson"
"managed cross functional teams"   "strong communication skills"
"leadership skills"   "expert presenter"
"Assisted with"   "worked with"
"helped with"   "top ranked"
"Increased revenue by"   "Exceeded goals by"
"decreased costs by"   "Exceeded quotas by"
"fast paced environment"   "company's bottom line"

INCLUDE: CUSTOM KEYWORDS & PHRASES

Make a list of keywords and phrases specific to your recruiting needs. To include the following:

Job Titles (that your company uses)
Job Titles (that your competition uses)
Competing Companies
Companies with similar technology
Schools (Your candidates attended)
Area Codes (for location specific requisitions)
Zip Codes (for location specific requisitions)
Associations
Acronyms
Degrees
Certifications
Alternative skill words from the job description
Skill words related to keywords in job description

Hmm...

How useful is this stuff if they can't apply it to their every day use?

I know! I will list a few search scenarios and share how I would resolve them. Yeah, that makes sense.

Below are a list of example search strings and the logic behind them. To apply them to your needs, simply change the word "keyword" in the search string to whatever keyword is relevant to your need. Also, change the word "job title" in the example below to the job title relevant to your search and so on. Add as many keywords as you like! Experiment, experiment, experiment. To assist you, the words I suggest you change are bolded.

Search strings are in blue and may extend beyond one line. Be careful to add the search into Google EXACTLY as written for the best results. Take note where words are touching a colon. For example, intitle:resume is how your search should be queried and **NOT** intitle: resume.

There are some cases where words are not touching a search command such as, when I use the "allintitle" command. For example: allintitle: planes trains automobiles That being said, pay very close attention to how I have written these examples. Cool? Cool.

I want to look for resumes where the authorship is claimed. For example, Alan Smith's resume. I also do not want to see examples of resumes. Neither do I want documents that have the word "submit" in them because that word is typically on a job description. For example, "if you are interested in this job, click here to submit your resume." Get it? This is how I would find resumes that meet my criteria.

intitle:"*'s resume" **keyword** -intitle:example -intitle:examples -intitle:sample -intitle:submit

I want to find curriculum vitaes. So, I look for terms related to curriculum vitae in the title of a document. I don't want job descriptions in my results, so I restrict the words "apply" and "submit" from being in any link. Why? More often than not, on a job description those words would be linking to a career page. I also don't want the word "jobs" in the title of a web document because that is a popular word in the title of career pages. I have also added the word "education" as that is a word that is on most resumes. (smile)

(intitle:curriculum.vitae OR inurl:vitae OR intitle:vitae) "**job title**" **keyword keyword** education -intitle:jobs -inanchor:apply -inanchor:submit

I am looking for resumes of college students in Atlanta who have a background in computer science. I do not want search results explaining how to do something in computer science, so I restrict the word "how" from the title of returned documents. For that matter, I do not want information about how to write a resume, so I restrict the word "write" from the title of returned documents . Finally, I restrict my search results to websites that end in "edu" because I want resumes that have been posted on a college server.

(intitle:"resume for" OR intitle:"resume of") **atlanta** **"computer science"** -inanchor:apply -inanchor:submit -inanchor:sample -intitle:how -intitle:write site:edu

I am looking for a Sales executive in Houston who is a great producer and who has managed teams. In the search string below, I am looking for a set of words that would be included on such a resume. Notice that I am using the **tilde** symbol in front of the word "executive" as I am looking not only for the word executive but words related to that as well. For example, words like: management and/or director.

allintext: (summary OR objective) education "leadership skills" "exceeded quota" sales **~executive** present houston

Below is another way I would seek out a Sales executive in Houston.

allintext: "increased revenue by" exceeded education (sales OR "business development") Houston (summary OR objective OR skills)

This is a third attempt to find a Sales person in Houston. Notice how I have the tilde in front of TX? This tells Google to find documents that cite various areas inside of TX. I have also added multiple area codes to the search as well. Why? Often people will add their phone numbers to their resumes.

intitle:resume sales ("exceeded quota" OR "proven track record" OR "bottom line") education **~TX (281 OR 713 OR 832)** email -intitle:sample -intitle:example

People also list their full address on their resumes from time to time as well. In the search below, I am using the numrange command to find results with zip codes that are based in Houston, TX.

77002..77012 intitle:resume sales quota

Forward!

Think you got the gist of it?

Well guess what? Surprise! There is a bit more to it. Let me share some tips on finding resumes your competition is overlooking.

When you don't know a web address, you automatically think (whatever the name is) dot com. Right? I do too. But, there are a lot of top level domains out there. And said domains, also contain resumes.

NOTE: GoDaddy sells hosting and domain registrations. Among the top level domains (TLD) they sell registration on are: .com, .net, .org, .us, .biz, .name and others.

TOP LEVEL DOMAINS

.COM	.NAME	.WS	.PRO	BIZ	. CC	.US.COM
.NET	.INFO	.COM.CO	.US	.ME	.TV	.EDU
.ORG	.CO	.NET.CO				

Above is a list of some top level domains you may want to experiment with for sourcing resumes. It is by no means an exhaustive list of options. Below are a three search string examples to get your creative juices flowing.

In the first search string, I am looking for the phrase "my resume" in a link on a web page or in the title. I am also excluding potential job descriptions and resume templates. Finally, I am limiting my search to documents on certain top level domains.

inanchor:my.resume **keyword "job title" city** education present -jobs -apply -submit -required -wanted -template -wizard -free -write -sample (site:net OR site:name OR site:org)

In the string below, I am looking for resumes that are formatted in either PDF or word document format. I am also limiting my search to documents on the .CC domain.

intitle:resume **"job title" "company name" keyword keyword** (filetype:pdf OR filetype:doc) -jobs -apply -submit -required -wanted -write -sample site:cc

By the way, every country has a top level domain. For example, .AU is the top level domain for Australia. So, by restricting search results to documents on that domain, I could target resumes hosted in Australia.

site:au intitle:vitae **keyword keyword keyword** education -inanchor:submit -inanchor:apply ext:pdf

NOTE: You can find a list of country-specific top level domains at: www.iana.org/domains/root/db

RESUME SPELLINGS

Did you know that there is more than one way to spell "resume?" Different spellings will result in different search results. Check out the searches I did below and the results.

intitle:**resume** programmer education -sample -your -apply -template [840,000 results]

intitle:**résumé** programmer education -sample -your -apply -template [13,700 results]

intitle:**resumé** programmer education -sample -your -apply -template [2,310 results]

RESUME WRITERS

Resume Writers tend to use common formats when crafting work histories. Their customers tend not to make changes to the documents and upload them to the web as is. Such being the case, a search for certain resume formats will yield results that are often overlooked.

intitle:elegant.resume   education **keyword keyword** present (ext:doc | ext:pdf) -inanchor:submit -inanchor:apply -intext:sample -intext:apply

intitle:functional.resume   education **keyword keyword** present (ext:doc | ext:pdf) -inanchor:submit -inanchor:apply -intext:sample -intext:apply

intitle:academic.resume   education **keyword keyword keyword** present (ext:doc | ext:pdf) -inanchor:submit -inanchor:apply -intext:sample -intext:apply

intitle:chronological.resume   **keyword keyword** education present (ext:doc | ext:pdf) -inanchor:submit -inanchor:apply -intext:sample -intext:apply

ACRONYMS

Some candidates do not list acronyms on their resumes but instead, spell out the abbreviation fully. Case in point, check out the different results between these two searches. Below I am looking for the phrase "extensible markup language" on a resume or vitae but, I do not want the keyword "xml" to appear on the resume. I find only a few resumes this way but, they were most likely overlooked previously by my competition.

(intitle:vitae OR intitle:resume) education extensible.markup.language -xml -apply -submit -sample -template [23 results]

When I seek out resumes with the acronym "XML" and restrict documents that contain the phrase it stands for, I get many more. Oh! By the way, I asked Google to restrict documents that had XML in the title as well as I was getting results I did not want. Go figure.

(intitle:vitae OR intitle:resume) education intext:XML -extensible.markup.language -intitle:xml -apply -submit -sample -template [16,200 results]

Let's try a similar search, shall we? Just to bring this point on home. When I look for "Microsoft Office Sharepoint Server" on a resume and restrict reference to its common acronym "MOSS," I only get a few results.

(intitle:vitae OR intitle:resume) education "microsoft office sharepoint server" -MOSS -apply -submit -sample -template [83 results]

Of course, the inverse brings back what I expected, lots and lots more resumes in comparison. Be advised that I added the keyword "sharepoint" in the search below. Why? I was getting a lot of resumes from people whose name was "Moss." Adding sharepoint to the mix did not wholly cancel that out but, it did give me more of what I wanted to see. Just fyi...

(intitle:vitae OR intitle:resume) education MOSS sharepoint -microsoft.office.sharepoint.server -apply -submit -sample -template [148,000 results]

Natural Language

Another way to find passive candidates is not to look for resumes but instead, look for phrases said online. You might be amazed by the number of people you can find with this technique. Think about it. How many people are online talking about the work they do on their blog or inside of a forum? Below are a few things I found when I searched on **"I work at Google."**

Dan Russell's Home Page & Site
sites.google.com/site/dmrussell/
I work at Google. I write. I analyze. I experiment. I do field studies and I try to understand what makes Google users tick. Why do they sometimes query Google for ...

Life at Google – The Microsoftie Perspective | Just Say \"No\" To ...
no2google.wordpress.com/.../life-at-google-the-microsoftie-perspecti...
Jun 24, 2007 – I used to work at Microsoft, now **I work at Google**. Much in this post is accurate, but mostly it is irrelevant. Engineers join Google and love ...

I work at Google and want to refer software engineers. Anyone ...
www.reddit.com/r/.../**i_work_at_google**_and_want_to_refer_softwar...
Nov 19, 2012 – I'm looking to refer software engineers for the NY office. I figure I spend a lot of time on Reddit so maybe there are other people like me on here.

Mike Stay - Google+ - I work at Google on the Caja project [1] and I ...
https://plus.google.com/.../posts/VxXav78ZDpm

by Mike Stay - in 810 Google+ circles - More by Mike Stay
Dec 15, 2012 – **I work at Google** on the Caja project [1] and I'm a PhD student at U. of Auckland. Cris Calude and John Baez (at UC Riverside) are my advisors; ...

Of course, this is only one example,. On the next page, I share several other search methods you might want to experiment with. Enjoy...

Try the following searches on Google. Change the bolded keywords to keywords that are relevant to whatever type of candidate you are seeking to recruit.

CANDIDATES DISCUSSING THEIR WORK

"I am a **job title**"
"I graduated from **school**" **keyword**
"I work in a **keyword**" lab
"I work at **company name**"
"I love **company name**"
"I hate **company name**"
"I reported to * " "at work"
"We have been working on * for years"

COMPANIES BRAGGING ABOUT THEIR EMPLOYEES

"she has extensive experience in" **keyword**
"he has extensive experience in" **keyword phrase**
("he is" OR "she is") "subject matter expert" **keyword**
" * has been researching * for * years"

EXPERTS SHARING THEIR EXPERTISE

"about the author" **keyword**
"about the writer" **keyword phrase**
"is the author of * " **keyword**
" * has written several " **keyword**

NOTE: This is one of my favorite search strategies! Just sayin'... One thing I have noticed about using wildcards in your natural language search is that you can have up to **3** wildcards in a search. Any more than that and you get nothing back in return. And it typically works best when your search is in quotes. For example...

"I developed * software for * and * mobile devices"

UGH!

Duh!

I almost forgot to share something with you concerning search. Glad I remembered.

Of course, you wouldn't have known if I didn't just tell you. Double duh!

In the search string below, I am looking for an old resume of a PhD student well-versed in oncology. Why an old one? Well, for one, less competition as most recruiters are only looking for new ones. For two, since fewer recruiters are looking for them, maybe the candidate won't feel so hassled when I call. For three, I am taking an educated guess that this might be a perfect candidate for my needs now if they were at a certain point in their career back then. (wink) But, I digress...

After doing the search below, I want more options to explore. Just beneath the search box is a link called "Search Tools" that you might not have paid much attention to in the past. (See the arrow pointing to it?)

Google   (1997-present OR 2002-present) university.of.* oncology PhD ext:pdf

Web   Images   Maps   Shopping   More ▾   Search tools

About 241,000 results (0.27 seconds)

[PDF] THE NEW JERSEY COMMISSION ON **CANCER** RESEARCH ...
www.state.nj.us/health/ccr/documents/ppgroups.pdf
File Format: PDF/Adobe Acrobat - Quick View
UMD-New Jersey Medical School. 1986-1987. S. J. Flint, **PhD**. Princeton **University**.
1994-1997. David Gold, **PhD**. Garden State **Cancer** Center. **1997-present** ...

[PDF] to Download - The **University of Texas** Health Science Center at ...
www.uthouston.edu/dotAsset/1355125.pdf
File Format: PDF/Adobe Acrobat - Quick View
2002-present Member of the **Graduate** Faculty, **Graduate** School of Biomedical
Sciences,. The **University of Texas** M. D. Anderson **Cancer** Center, Houston, TX ...

[PDF] Download CV/Biosketch - Fox Chase **Cancer** Center
www.fccc.edu/research/pid/fourkal/cv_fourkal_WEB.pdf
File Format: PDF/Adobe Acrobat - Quick View
1995-1999: **University of Saskatchewan Graduate** Scholarship ... Annual short course
on Monte Carlo treatment planning (**2002-present**). • Taught ...

Clicking that link causes three additional links to appear: **a)** Any Time, **b)** All Results and **c)** Search near. By clicking the "Any Time" link, I can refine my search results to those web pages that Google has found in the past hour, past 24 hours, past week, etc. (see opposite page) If I wanted to find results that Google added to its database in the past 24 hours, I would choose the "Past 24 Hours" link. By the way, I often refine my searches to past week or so when looking for fresh resumes. Just fyi...

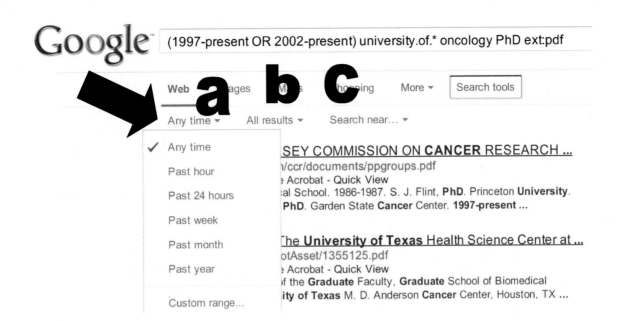

Check out the "All results" link. Clicking that link will bring more opportunities to refine your search. Among the choices is "Sites with Images" which can be very handy when sourcing diversity candidates. (Just a suggestion...) Let's take a closer look at this option.

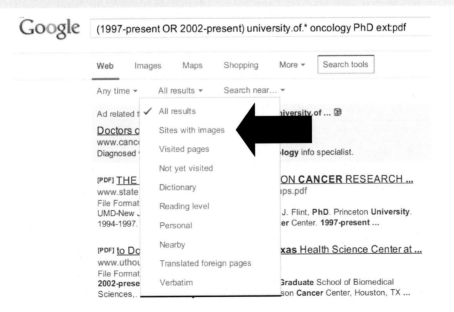

"meet the team" auto industry CTO

| Web | Images | Maps | Shopping | More ▼ | Search tools |

Any time ▼   Sites with images ▼   Clear

Images for **"meet the team" auto industry CTO** - Report images

Leadership | Founders, Executives, Board Members
www.dealer.com/company/leadership/

Meet the team behind the automotive marketing and operations leader - from ... sales and service experience in the **auto industry**, which includes 14 years as CEO .... Gibbs served as president and **CTO**, where he orchestrated a new phase in ... 6 images

DoublePositive :: **Meet the Team**
www.doublepositive.com/meet-our-team/

I would not use the **"Sites with Images"** refinement to find resumes. I would however use it to find people featured on company websites. (smile) In this example, I am looking for a CTO who works in the auto industry. Once I have a name, the company page will (no doubt) give me a phone number I can. How easy is that?

Google   (1997-present OR 2002-present) university.of.* oncology PhD ext:pdf   🎤   🔍

Web   Images   Maps   Shopping   More ▾   Search tools

Any time ▾   Related searches ▾   Clear

Related searches for **(1997-present OR 2002-present) university.of.***
oncology PhD ext:pdf:

1997 present 2002 present university of * oncology phd **curriculum vitae**
1997 present 2002 present university of * oncology phd **associate professor**
1997 present 2002 present university of * oncology phd **biosketch**
1997 present 2002 present university of * oncology phd **clinic**
1997 present 2002 present university of * oncology phd **faculty**

[PDF] to Download - The **University of Texas** Health Science Center at ...
www.uthouston.edu/dotAsset/1355125.pdf
File Format: PDF/Adobe Acrobat - Quick View
2002-present Member of the **Graduate** Faculty, **Graduate** School of Biomedical
Sciences,. The **University of Texas** M. D. Anderson **Cancer** Center, Houston, TX ...

[PDF] curriculum vitae - Radiation **Oncology** at UTHSCSA - The **Univer**...
radonc.uthscsa.edu/Doctors/YuaneCV.pdf
File Format: PDF/Adobe Acrobat - Quick View
Aug 21, 2008 – Head Instructor. OTHER TEACHING: 01/**2002 - Present** Guest
Professor, **Cancer** Center, Sun. Yet-sen **University**, China. **Cancer** Center, Sun ...

[PDF] Download CV/Biosketch - Fox Chase **Cancer** Center
www.fccc.edu/research/pid/fourkal/cv_fourkal_WEB.pdf
File Format: PDF/Adobe Acrobat - Quick View
1995-1999: **University of Saskatchewan Graduate** Scholarship ... Annual short
course on Monte Carlo treatment planning (**2002-present**). • Taught ...

[PDF] James Balter, Ph.D. - Regents of the **University of Michigan**
www.regents.umich.edu/.../Radiation%20O**ncology**/Balter,%20James...
File Format: PDF/Adobe Acrobat - Quick View
2002—Present Associate Professor of Radiation **Oncology**, **University of**. Michigan
... undergraduate and **graduate** student research projects and fellowships.

Returning to my previous search for a PhD student for a moment, by choosing the refinement of
"Related searches," Google suggests more keywords and phrases I can search on based on what I am
presently searching. (As indicative by the arrow above.)

(1997-present OR 2002-present) university.of.* oncology PhD ext:pdf   🎤 Jim

Web   Images   Maps   Shopping   More ▼ | Search tools |

Any time ▼   Reading level ▼   Clear

Ad related to **(1997-present OR 2002-present) university.of** ... 🔲

Doctors of **Oncology**   1 (877) 530 5322
www.cancercenter.com/
Diagnosed with cancer? Chat online with an **oncology** info specialist.

Results by reading level for **(1997-present OR 2002-present) university.of.* oncology PhD ext:pdf**:

Basic   < 1%   ▮
Intermediate   6%   ▬▬
Advanced   93%   ▬▬▬▬▬▬▬▬▬▬▬▬▬▬▬▬▬▬▬▬

[PDF] THE NEW JERSEY COMMISSION ON **CANCER** RESEARCH ...
www.state.nj.us/health/ccr/documents/ppgroups.pdf
File Format: PDF/Adobe Acrobat - Quick View
Advanced reading level
UMD-New Jersey Medical School. 1986-1987. S. J. Flint, **PhD**. Princeton **University**.
1994-1997. David Gold, **PhD**. Garden State **Cancer** Center. **1997-present** ...

[PDF] to Download - The **University of Texas** Health Science Center at ...
www.uthouston.edu/dotAsset/1355125.pdf
File Format: PDF/Adobe Acrobat - Quick View
2002-present Member of the **Graduate** Faculty, **Graduate** School of Biomedical
Sciences,. The **University of Texas** M. D. Anderson **Cancer** Center, Houston, TX ...

[PDF] Download CV/Biosketch - Fox Chase **Cancer** Center
www.fccc.edu/research/pid/fourkal/cv_fourkal_WEB.pdf
File Format: PDF/Adobe Acrobat - Quick View
Advanced reading level
1995-1999: **University of Saskatchewan Graduate** Scholarship ... Annual short course

By refining the search by "Reading level" I am able to sift the results by, well... reading level. It makes sense that most of these results are on an advanced reading level since I am looking for a PhD. I don't use this refinement much but when I do, my assumption is that this search returns more learned candidates. Or rather, the ones that use fancier terms.   ;-)

(1997-present OR 2002-present) university.of.* oncology PhD ext:pdf

Web   Images   Maps   Shopping   More ▾   Search tools

Any time ▾   **Nearby** ▾   City ▾   Atlanta, GA ▾   Clear

[PDF] CURRICULUM VITAE 7 - Emory Healthcare
www.emoryhealthcare.org/medical.../caliendo-cv-09signed.pd...
File Format: PDF/Adobe Acrobat - Quick View
School of Medicine, Atlanta, GA. **2002 - present** Associate Professor, Medicine, Emory
University School of Medicine, Atlanta, ... Angela M. Caliendo, MD, **PhD** 2 ... Advisor:
Mulchand S. Patel, **PhD**. 1987 MD. **.... 1997 - present**. 2000 - **......** **Cancer** Symposium,
The **University of Texas** MD Anderson **Cancer** Center, Houston, TX.

[PDF] (format for NHW School of Nursing) - Emory **University** School of ...
www.nursing.emory.edu/directory/assets/.../sdonaldson-CV.pd...
File Format: PDF/Adobe Acrobat - Quick View
1973 **PhD**. **University of Washington**, Seattle, WA. Physiology & Biophysics. 1967
Post- **.....** Member of External Advisory Committee **2002-present**. Southern ...

[PDF] Spring 2010 (Vol. 120 No. 2) (PDF) - Spelman College: Home
www5.spelman.edu/about.../SpelmanMessengerSpring2010.pd...
File Format: PDF/Adobe Acrobat - Quick View

Choosing the "Nearby" link **(a)** switches things up a bit. An additional option appears where you can refine your results by City **(b)**, State or Region. My IP address tipped Google off to my location as Atlanta, Ga. However, by clicking "Atlanta, GA" **(c)** I can change that to whatever city I want. This is a great tool for finding local talent! You see in the results the resumes found are from Emory and Spelman which are colleges in Atlanta.

 (1997-present OR 2002-present) university.of.* oncology PhD ext:pdf 🎤 Jim Str

| Web | Images | Maps | Shopping | More ▼ | Search tools |

Any time ▼   Translated foreign pages ▼   Clear

Translated results for **(1997-present OR 2002-present) university.of.* oncology PhD ext:pdf** - My language: English ▼

Language	Translated query	
Italian ✖	**(1997-oggi 2002-oggi) university.of. * Oncologia dottorato ext:pdf** - Edit	4,060 results
Spanish ✖	**(1997-presente 2002-actualidad) university.of. * Oncología PhD ext:pdf** - Edit	1,380 results
French ✖	**(1997-aujourd'hui 2002-présent) university.of. * Oncologie doctorat ext:pdf** - Edit	1,080 results
German ✖	**(1997-Gegenwart 2002-present) university.of. * Onkologie PhD ext:pdf** - Edit	298 results

Add language ▼

[PDF] Science curriculum - **University of Bergamo**
www.unibg.it/dati/persone/1505/6298.pdf
File Format: PDF/Adobe Acrobat - Quick View
Translated from: Italian
Date curriculum. November 2012. 1) Personal data. Year of birth. Name and surname. **University** service. March 11, 1971. Stefano Tomelleri. **University of...**
+ Show original text

[PDF] CV - Regenerative Surgery
www.regenerativesurgery.it/third/faculty/cv/Gaspari.pdf
File Format: PDF/Adobe Acrobat - Quick View
Translated from: Italian
1. CURRICULUM VITAE. Achille L. Gaspari, MD Born in Rome October 16, 1946.
Professor and Chairman, General Surgery, **University of Rome** Tor Vergata...
+ Show original text

[PDF] Curriculum Vitae - **University of Urbino**
www.uniurb.it/biotecnologie/didattica/docenti/.../CVBoiani.pdf

Refining my results to "Translated foreign pages" comes in handy when looking for candidates in other countries. By clicking the "Add language" link (see arrow above) I am able to translate to even more languages. Very cool feature Google.

(1997-present OR 2002-present) university.of.* oncoology student

Web | Images | Maps | Shopping | More ▼ | Search tools

Any time ▼ | **Verbatim** ▼ | Clear

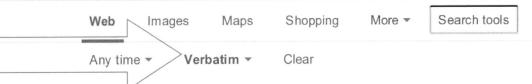

Did you mean: (1997-present OR 2002-present) university.of.* *oncology* student

[DOC] curriculum vitae - University of Oklahoma Health Sciences Center
www.ouhsc.edu/benbrooklab/Benbrook-cv.doc
File Format: Microsoft Word - Quick View
1997- present Associate Professor and Director of Research .... Editor Cancer Epidemiology, Biomarkers & Prevention, **2002-present**. ... Reviewer for University Grants Committee, **University of** Hong Kong, 2006 ... **Student** Admissions and Recruitment Committee, 2004-2005 ..... Gynecologic **Oncoology**, 73: 253-256. 22.

Program for the st International conference for treatment of
www.docstoc.com/.../Program-for-the-st-International-confere...
... Lancet **Oncoology**, Digestive Surgery, Hepato-Gastroenterology, Endoscopy, ... **University of Pennsylvania**-School of Medicine Curriculum Vitae March 7, 2008 ... **2002- present** Assistant Professor **University of Pennsylvania**, Philadelphia of ..... **student** ·National Yan-Ming University, Taipei, Taiwan 1988-1995 College of ...

CURRICULUM VITAE 637 views - SlideShare
www.slideshare.net/terrybear11/curriculum-vitae-5606484
Oct 29, 2010 – ... Section **University of Oklahoma** College of Medicine **1997-present** Adjunct Associate ... present Co-Director, Gynecologic Cancer Program **2002 – present** Scientific Review ... Dental/Pharmacy Course Curriculum Committee, 2003-2004 **Student** Admissions and ..... Gynecologic **Oncoology**, 73: 253-256.

The "Verbatim" searches for exactly what you are looking for and does not include synonyms or related terms based on what it thinks you are looking for. In this example, I am looking for a student who has misspelled the word "oncology" on their resume. Definitely a small number of candidates but, candidates that have been overlooked by my competitors as well.

NEXT?

Hmm...

I wonder if they know about the other resources on Google that can be leveraged for sourcing purposes?

Google books

Researching a topic?

Search the latest index of the world's books. Find millions of great books you can preview or read for free.

| pediatric sonography | **Search Books** |

Browse books and magazines »

New! Shop for Books on Google Play

Browse the world's largest eBookstore and start reading today on the web, tablet, phone, or ereader.

Google play

My library

books.google.com

I want to take you through a demo of how I would use **Google Books** to find passive candidates. In this example, I am looking for someone with a background in pediatric sonography. The strategy is simple enough. Basically, I look for books on the subject and then focus on who the author is. If they can write a book on the subject, I can assume that they are an expert and quite possibly, someone I want to recruit. Make sense?

To get to Google Books, I go to the address above: http://books.google.com

Google   pediatric sonography   🎤 Jim S

Web   Images   Maps   Shopping   **Books**   More ▾   Search tools

About 58,700 results (0.52 seconds)

Pediatric Sonography

books.google.com/books?isbn=1451153228
Marilyn J. Siegel - 2011 - Preview - More editions
This edition features more than 1,800 clear, sharp images, including over 300 full-color images throughout.

Pediatric Ultrasound: How, Why and When

books.google.com/books?isbn=0080982484
Rose de Bruyn, Kassa Darge - 2010 - Preview - More editions
This book addresses the 'how', 'why' and 'when' of pediatric ultrasound. Each chapter begins with the 'how': how to scan and what special techniques or tricks to use when scanning children.

Practical **pediatric** imaging: diagnostic radiology of infants and ... - Page 60

books.google.com/books?isbn=0316494739
Donald R. Kirks, M.D., Nathan Thorne Griscom - 1998 - Preview - More editions
Increased renal cortical echogenicity in **pediatric** renal disease: histopathologic correlations. J Clin **Ultrasound** 1986;14:595-600. 121. Finkelstein MS, Rosenberg HK. Snyder HM III. Duckett JW. **Ultrasound** evaluation of scrotum in **pediatrics**.

When the results are returned, I click on the very first result because it came up in my eenie-meenie-minee-moe algorithm. (Pretty advanced science, huh?)

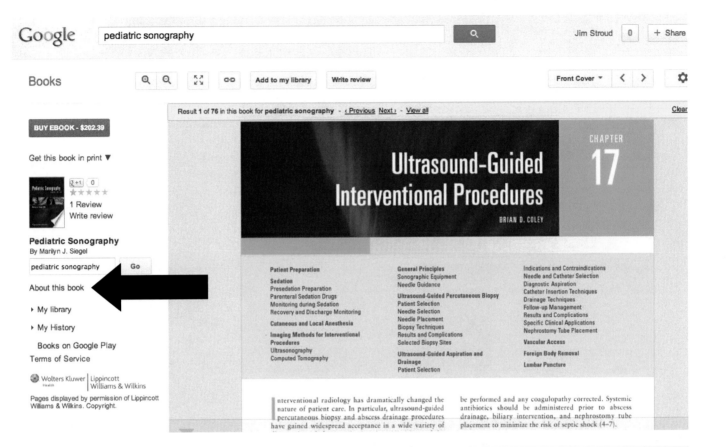

Google will take you to an excerpt of that book that features your keyword. Click the "About this Book" link on the left. (indicated by the arrow)

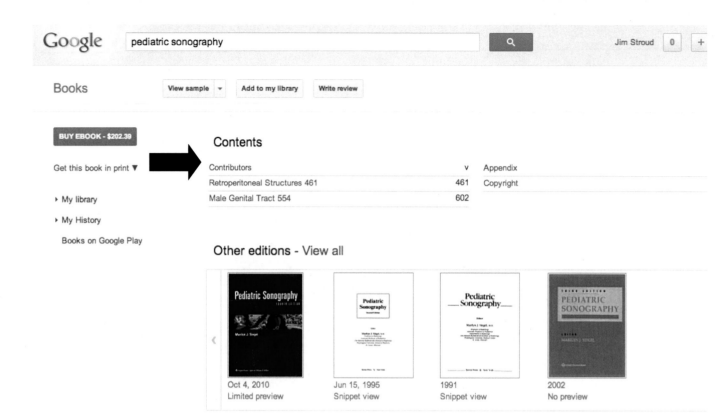

Scroll down the page until you see the "Contributors" section. Click that link. (as shown by the arrow)

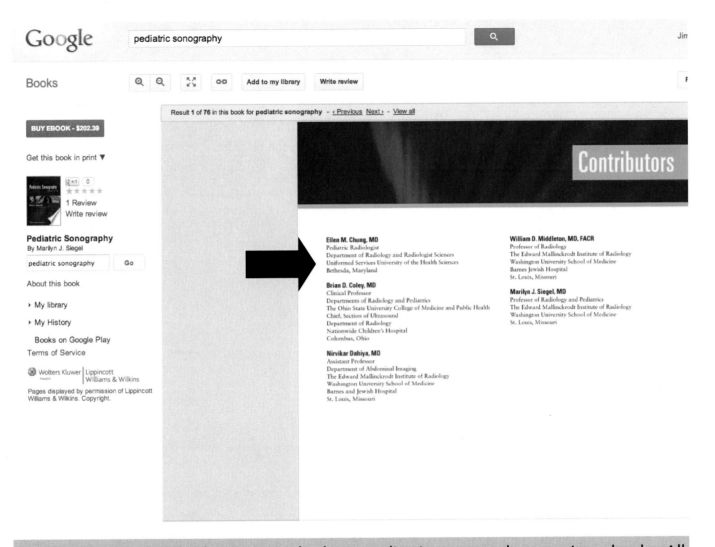

Contributors

Ellen M. Chung, MD
Pediatric Radiologist
Department of Radiology and Radiologist Sciences
Uniformed Services University of the Health Sciences
Bethesda, Maryland

Brian D. Coley, MD
Clinical Professor
Departments of Radiology and Pediatrics
The Ohio State University College of Medicine and Public Health
Chief, Section of Ultrasound
Department of Radiology
Nationwide Children's Hospital
Columbus, Ohio

Nirvikar Dahiya, MD
Assistant Professor
Department of Abdominal Imaging
The Edward Mallinckrodt Institute of Radiology
Washington University School of Medicine
Barnes and Jewish Hospital
St. Louis, Missouri

William D. Middleton, MD, FACR
Professor of Radiology
The Edward Mallinckrodt Institute of Radiology
Washington University School of Medicine
Barnes Jewish Hospital
St. Louis, Missouri

Marilyn J. Siegel, MD
Professor of Radiology and Pediatrics
The Edward Mallinckrodt Institute of Radiology
Washington University School of Medicine
St. Louis, Missouri

Voila! Five people who know enough about pediatric sonography to write a book. All books do not have a contributor section but most likely have an "About the Author" section where there is some biographical information. In many cases, these sections cite where they are currently working. (wink)

Good luck!

google.com/videohp

I want to take you through a demo of how I would use **Google Videos** to find passive candidates. And just as a side note, searching Google Video has its advantages over searching YouTube in that Google Video searches multiple video sites (YouTube included).

Google   "he is a software engineer"

Web   Images   Maps   Shopping   **Videos**   More ▾   Search tools

About 474,000 results (0.15 seconds)

Software Engineer Sound Clip and Quote - Hark

www.hark.com/a/clips/dwtlbstczl-software-engineer
Mar 14, 2013
Jasmine asks for some clarification when Jesse tells the beauties
that **he is a software engineer**. Related to ...

Software Engineer Sound Clip and Quote - Hark

www.hark.com/clips/dwtlbstczl-software-engineer
Feb 5, 2011
Jasmine asks for some clarification when Jesse tells the beauties
that **he is a software engineer**. Related to ...

Leon Alphans Traille Jr., Ballston Mall Molotov cocktail suspect, charg...

www.wjla.com/.../leon-alphans-traille-jr-ballston-mall-...
Oct 19, 2012
He says on his linkedin site that **he is a software engineer** with a
master's degree in computer science from ...

Cubox · Our Crew

cuboxlabs.com/people/
Jan 24, 2012

I search Google Video using natural language search. I just try to imagine phrases someone might say that would interest me from a sourcing point of view. For example, I can
hear someone introducing someone on camera. Say... John Doe, he is a software
engineer and he will be reviewing this product. (Or something more or less like that,
which is the reasoning behind the search above.)

 "he is the CTO of * "

Web   Images   Maps   Shopping   **Videos**   More ▾   Search tools

About 1,100,000 results (0.49 seconds)

Elon Musk | CEO of SpaceX and Tesla Motors | Big Think

bigthink.com/users/elonmusk
Jan 24, 2012
**He is currently the CEO and CTO of SpaceX, CEO and Product
Architect** of Tesla Motors and Chairman of ...

Startup Grind 2013 Hosts Tom Conrad (Pandora) - YouTube

▶ 26:10

www.youtube.com/watch?v=MfaDMK5iERI
Feb 24, 2013 - Uploaded by StartupGrind
After such an interesting history, it would only make sense that
today **he is the CTO of Pandora. Learn more ...**

What's wrong with Wi-Fi? by Dave Täht - YouTube

▶ 57:45

www.youtube.com/watch?v=Wksh2DPHCDI
Feb 15, 2013 - Uploaded by Keith Winstein
He is the CTO of Teklibre, LLC, and associated with the LINCS
lab in Paris and the Internet Systems ...

Defcon 19: Panel - Represent! Defcon Groups, Hackerspaces, and Yo...

▶ 47:34

www.youtube.com/watch?v=Z-ZLiYR6P4A
Mar 14, 2012 - Uploaded by SecurityTubeCons
Meanwhile, **he is the CTO of Security Art and co-founder** of
DC9723. In his former life, he was a Software ...

Data Driven Decisions - Ben Curren - YouTube

▶ 56:54

www.youtube.com/watch?v=trbOW1TDOao
Dec 13, 2012 - Uploaded by GaslightLive
... products that improve the lives of small businesses. **He
currently is the Founder and CTO of Outright.com ...**

On the previous page, I show an example of a search I am doing for a CTO. The great thing about searching Google Videos is that I can find where executives are being interviewed about their company or a topic related to their company. Below are a few more searches you might want to experiment with. Where you see the word "keyword" or "keyword phrase," simply change to something relevant to your recruiting needs.

" * is the CTO of * " **keyword**
" he is the CFO of * " **keyword phrase**
" she has extensive experience in * " **keyword**
" (he OR she) has created * for the * industry" **keyword**
"as a "**job title**" (he OR she) * "
 " * was recently promoted to * " **keyword**
" (he OR she OR they) developed a process * " **keyword**
" * was instrumental in * " **keyword**

As I think about it, these searches would also work well on Google Blog Search.

google.com/blogsearch

Web   Images   Maps   Shopping   **Blogs**   More ▾   Search tools

About 234,000 results (0.90 seconds)

Blog homepages for " *** is the CTO of *** "

Unplugged Development
www.unpluggeddevelopment.com/
Miguel is the CTO of Xamarin, and the director of the Mono Project. A few points from his talk follow: ...

Ciaran Rooney on Zerply
ciaran.ie/
Ciarán is the CTO of Skimlinks where he leads the technical innovation for Skimlinks' products and the platform's ...

IT Directions
www.ebizq.net/blogs/it_directions/
Keith is the CTO of Role Modellers Ltd, whose company mission is to develop understanding and support of ...

Bonobos' SF Engineers Split Between NY Relocation And New ...
techcrunch.com/
Mar 29, 2013 by Jordan Crook
Michael Hart is the CTO of Bonobos, the largest, born-online apparel brand in the US. Before his current role, Michael led engineering for Netflix's social program and created their API, which today supports over a hundred ...
More results from TechCrunch

TECHdotMN — Meet a Minnesota CTO: Ben Nielsen
tech.mn/
Mar 29, 2013 by sourced

See what I mean? Above is a search on blogs for people who have been introduced as a CTO of a certain company. This works great, but its not the only way I would source from blogs.

 intitle:about.me programmer

Web   Images   Maps   Shopping   **Blogs**   More ▾   Search tools

About 2,140 results (0.38 seconds)

ZettaZete – **About Me**

zettazete.com/
Mar 7, 2013 by ZettaZete
I am truly addicted to **programming**, truly addicted. It is nearly 90% of what I do each
day. I am extremely fast at learning, so I adapt to my task at hand. Right now I don't
have much to brag about in my **programming** career.

Andy Kilner - General purpose **programmer** of general purpose ...

andykilner.co.uk/
Jan 8, 2010 by gnublade
View Andy Kilner on about.me. About.me makes it easy for you to learn about Andy
Kilner's background and interests.
- References

About Me | Programmer 4 Life

Bloggers (more often than not) have an "About Me" section where they will cite their
professional background. In this search, I am looking for "About Me" info and adding the word
"programmer" to find bloggers who describe themselves as Programmers. If not that, at least they
have that word on their self-description.

FYI, other searches you might want to try on Google Blog Search are:

intitle:my.profile **keyword**

intitle:profile ("contact me" OR "email me" OR "call me at") **keyword**

Google™ "I developed hardware for * " Jir

Web   Images   Maps   Shopping   More ▾   Search tools

About 759 results (0.27 seconds)

	Videos
	News
	Books

Jayesh Naik | LinkedIn
www.linkedin.com/in/jayeshnaik
Houston, Texas Area - Senior Engineering Profe   Places   ) Graphics
I developed Hardware for Embedded System   te Analog ...
Processor. I designed and developed VHDL bas   Blogs

Amazon.com: 2-Port KVM with Cables   Flights   s
www.amazon.com › ... › Computer Compon
Rating: 2.3 - 19 reviews - $28.00 - I   Discussions
I developed hardware for an international co   lue of a Design
Verification Test. Read more. Published on Mar   Recipes   3 ...

Replace Civic 96-98 heater control pan   Applications   el - Page 2
www.mp3car.com › ... › Mp3Car Technical H   Patents   ion
10 posts - 4 authors - Sep 5, 2005
Thats why i developed hardware for the climate control - its also easier and more
reliable to interface the pc to the device, and let the device do ...

Magnetized Target Fusion - Engineering - Science Forums
www.scienceforums.net › Sciences › Engineering
1 post - 1 author - Aug 3, 2011
... with a precision around 100μs using actuators that had 20ms response time, at a
company where I developed hardware for crash-test.

is General Fusion and Magnetized target fusion legit?

Natural language searching is also great when it comes to searching "Discussions." When you refine your search results by "Discussions," you are asking Google to concentrate the search to online forums.

 news feed optimization

Web   Images   Maps   Shopping   Videos   More ▾   Search tools

20 personal results. 15,400,000 other results.

News

Books

Places

Blogs

Flights

Discussions

Recipes

Applications

Patents

Ad related to **news feed optimization** 🔲

Data **Feed Optimization** - **Optimize** your Shoppin
www.single**feed**.com/
Improve CTR and Conversion Rate

PostRocket's '**News Feed Optimization**' For Face   ed ...
www.forbes.com/.../postrockets-**news-feed-optimizati**.

 by Tomio Geron - in 407 Google+ circles - More by
May 31, 2012 – If Facebook is a must for brand ma   eed
Optimization may be the next big thing.

BrandGlue: The **News Feed Optimization** Agenc
brandglue.com/
We pioneered using NFO (**Newsfeed Optimization**) to rank fan pages higher in the
Facebook algorithm. For every 100,000 fans, we can generate up to 1.5 ...

Marketers Try to Master Facebook's **Feed** | MIT Technology Review
www.technologyreview.com/**news**/.../marketers-try-t...

by Jessica Leber - in 90 Google+ circles - More by Jessica Leber
Jun 18, 2012 – This could also be the basis for a new growth industry. "**News
feed optimization** is still at its early stages. I'd compare it to search in 2001,"
says ...

And while I am looking at further ways to refine searches, one option I want to steer you towards is the "Patents" search. In the example above, I am looking up the term "News Feed Optimization." I choose "Patents" from under the "More" link.

 news feed optimization Ji

Web   Images   Maps   Shopping   **Patents**   More ▾   Search tools

About 2,290 results (0.41 seconds)

Adaptive ranking of **news feed** in social networking systems

 www.google.com/patents/US20130031034
App. - Filed Jul 29, 2011 - Published Jan 31, 2013 - Max Gubin -
Wayne, Vickrey David, Maykov Alexey
Machine learning models are used for ranking **news feed** stories ... a model based
on **optimization** of different types of ranking models, ...
Overview - Related - Discuss

News feed ranking model based on social information of viewer

 www.google.com/patents/US20130031489
App. - Filed Jul 29, 2011 - Published Jan 31, 2013 - Max Gubin - Gubin Max, Kao
Wayne, Vickrey David, Maykov Alexey
Machine learning models are used for ranking **news feed** stories ... a model based
on **optimization** of different types of ranking models, ...
Overview - Related - Discuss

Optimizing Feed Mixer Performance In A Paraffinic Froth Treatment ...

 www.google.com/patents/US20120279824
App. - Filed Jul 20, 2012 - Published Nov 8, 2012 - Michael F. Raterman -
Raterman Michael F, Sharma Arun K
Another process provides for **optimizing** the design of a bitumen froth treatment
plant by **optimizing** the diameter of the **feed** pipe to impart an optimum shear rate
...
Overview - Related - Discuss

In the search results you can see the names of those who applied for the patent. If they are skilled enough in something to file a patent for it, maybe you might want to hire them? (Smile) In a lot of cases you can see where they worked because the patent is filed on behalf of a company. If the name of the company is not revealed, further research will be necessary. (Maybe they are on LinkedIn?)

"is a software engineer at * "

Web   Images   Maps   Shopping   More ▾   Search tools

About 5,470,000 results (0.54 seconds)

| Videos |
| News |
| Books |

Brett Slatkin | CrunchBase Profile
www.crunchbase.com › People
Brett Slatkin **is a software engineer at Google**   **ing** lead on Google
Consumer Surveys. He formerly worked.

| Places |
| Blogs |

James S. Larson - Research at Google
research.google.com/pubs/author38117.htm
Jim Larson **is a Software Engineer at Google.**   **worked** at Jet
Propulsion Laboratory, Sendmail Inc., and Ama   is the ...

| Flights |
| Discussions |
| Recipes |

[PDF] Lun Xiao **is a software engineer a**   **er family** hav...
cafanc.org/election/election_2012/Lun_Xiao
File Format: PDF/Adobe Acrobat - Quick View
Lun Xiao **is a software engineer at IBM. Lun a**   ived in the RTP
area for. 17 years. During this time, she has participated in many community ...

| Applications |
| Patents |

Comet Daily » Alex Russell
cometdaily.com/people/alex_russell/
Alex Russell **is a software Engineer at Google working on Chrome Frame**. He
serves as President of the Dojo Foundation, an organization that supports ...

Aman Varshney profiles | LinkedIn
www.linkedin.com/pub/dir/Aman/Varshney
Particularly interested in client/server and cloud applications. Aman Varshney **is a
software engineer at Nine Dot Nine Mediaworx Pvt** Ltd. Aman Varshney ...

In this example, I am looking for the mention of someone working as a software engineer at some company. I refine my search by "News," as shown above, by clicking the "News" link (indicated by the arrow).

Google privacy director steps down after three years
ITProPortal - Apr 2, 2013
... You in June. You **is currently a software engineer at Google, and will take on**
'director of privacy for product and engineering' as his new title.

Computerworld

Google slashes Nik plug-in suite pricing, making amends for ...
imaging resource - by Mike Tomkins - Mar 25, 2013
Pesch was formerly the development manager at Nik Software, and **is now a**
manager and software engineer at Google. In his post, he reveals ...

Economic Ti...

Apple Just Missed This Acquisition
Motley Fool - Mar 15, 2013
Apple exec Eddy Cue's son Adam Cue **is a software engineer at Mailbox's parent**
company, which made this union seemingly likely. Previously ...

RAHS National Merit Finalists announced
Lillie News - Mar 12, 2013
They were both engineering professors in China and her mother **is a software engineer at 3M in**
Maplewood. "My mother and grandparents ...

Stay up to date on these results:
- Create an email alert for **"is a software engineer at * "**

And in the search results, I see 3 recent articles citing software engineers in the news. More often that not, the company they work for will be cited in the article as well. (Yay!)

The added bonus about searching on Google News is that I can save my search as a Google Alert and get updates via email when new content hits the news that fits my interest. (see arrow) More on **Google Alerts** later.

Here are a few more natural language search suggestions for you to experiment with on Google News. As always, change "job title," "keyword" and "keyword phrase" to terms relevant to what you are looking for.

"new role as" ("**job title**" OR "**job title**" OR "**job title**")
"said her department will * " **keyword**
"said his group will * " **keyword**
"according to * " **keyword phrase**

[Care to do some competitive intel?]

" * said that **company** will * " intitle:**company.product**

[Who is laying off people you want to recruit?]

" * said that * will * " intitle:layoffs **keyword**

[Who is discussing sales trends in New York?]

intitle:sales ("he said" OR "She said" OR "according to") trends **source:**nytimes

[What is the next big thing ? Want to recruit an innovator?]

"patent pending technology" intitle:**keyword**

Okay at this point, I am wondering if I should continue with more data. On one hand, I've already given you a lot to digest and practice with. And on the other, I feel the search geek in me begging to unleash more data. Hmm... Shall I stop or "geek" out more?

At one point or another, it happens to all Sourcers and Recruiters. You've done all the boolean searching you know how to do and now, you feel stuck. This happens to me quite a bit and I welcome it because it encourages me to experiment. Its not difficult for me to get so consumed into a search and trying new things that I forget what I was looking for initially. (Yes, I really am a geek that way.) Case in point, let me share with you a thought process I had the other day.

I was training some recruiters and picked up on something I think most recruiters overlook. When looking for resumes, they tend to search exclusively for PDF documents or Microsoft Word documents. However, there are several filetype formats that are findable on the web. (Is "findable" a word?) And for that matter, are PDFs and DOCs the most popular file formats for resumes? I mean, I assume that because that's all I tend to see. But, is that really the case?

Time to geek! Excuse me as I mull things over in my mind.

Hmm... No matter what I search on, Google will give you at most 1,000 results. I should make some search strings that will show as many resumes as possible and that do not target any particular industry. I will then narrow those findings down by targeting resumes of various filetypes. Yeah, that makes sense. Right?

Hmm...

(intitle:resume.of   OR   intitle:resume.by   OR   intitle:resume.for   OR   intitle:my.resume   OR intitle:"*'s resume") inurl:resume (present OR current) (education OR university.of) -template -submit -apply -openings

In the above search, I am looking for a resume that will have (most likely) "resume of John Doe" OR "resume by John Doe" OR someone who has titled their resume "my resume" OR "John Doe's Resume") The results will have the term "resume" in the URL and words common on a resume like "present" or "current" and... I think you get it from here. (smile)

The end result was not a flood of resumes as I had hoped. There were a lot of articles about writing resumes and other such career related advice. However, I was pleased with what happened when I refined my search to focus on specific filetypes. For example, in the following search string, my focus is on resumes that are in PDF format. I do this by looking for documents that have "resume.pdf" in the URL. I bolded it below to make it easy to spot.

(intitle:resume.of OR intitle:resume.by OR intitle:resume.for OR intitle:my.resume OR intitle:"*'s resume") **inurl:resume.pdf** (present OR current) (education OR university.of) -template -submit -apply -openings

Based on the results from this and other search strings focused on other formats, the most popular resume formats are:

1) HTML   6) DOCX
2) HTM   7) SHTML
3) PHP   8) ASP
4) PDF   9) RTF
5) DOC   10) CGI

Hmm... That's interesting. I wonder which domains have the most resumes on them? If I wanted to gauge that, how would I? I suppose I would run a search (similar to the one I just did) and refine my searches by top level domain. Yeah, that makes sense. And since the most popular format for resumes is HTML, I will make that a focus as well. Let me show you what I mean, just to be sure I have not lost you.

(intitle:resume.of OR intitle:resume.by OR intitle:resume.for OR intitle:my.resume OR intitle:"*'s resume") **inurl:resume.html** (present   OR current) (education OR   university.of) -template -submit -apply -openings **site:info**

The above search string is looking for resumes as I have before. The only difference is , by adding "site:info" I am looking at results that are hosted on a .info domain. For example, notice the URL in the search result below.

Resume of Tomoko Adachi
astromoko.**info**/Resume.html
Education & Current Position: Engineer, Code 553. Detector System ...
Greenbelt, MD. Physics Department, Catholic University of America

Based on the results from this and other search strings , these are the top domains ranked by number of resumes hosted. **90%** were on the .COM domain. Zowie!

1) .COM   6) .INFO
2) .EDU   7) .US
3) .NET   8) .BIZ
4) .ORG   9) .ME
5) .WS   10) .CC

Most popular way resume is spelled online.
- Resume is the most popular way to spell resume.
- Resumé is the second most popular way to spell resume.
- Résumé is the third popular way to spell resume.

(Just in case you are wondering, I use the "Verbatim" refinement to look for exact spellings in the title of documents.)

And while I am on that subject... Wait! Did I answer the question I was trying to figure out initially? Let me flip back a couple of pages and see. (smile)

Ah! This all started around me suggesting things you can do when you get stuck on a search. Maybe I should just list a bunch of search strings for my readers to play with? I wonder if they would like that? Hm... Decisions, decisions, decisions... Let me think a sec'.

Hmmm... We're getting pretty close to the end of the book. I will... I know... Share a few cool tools that will help them manage all of the data they will find online. Yeah, good idea. Go with that.

Google

Web History

With Web History, you'll be able to:

View and manage your web activity.

You know that great web site you saw online and now can't find? From now on, you can. With Web History, you can view and search across the full text of the pages you've visited, including Google searches, web pages, images, videos and news stories. You can also manage your web activity and remove items from your web history at any time.

Get the search results most relevant to you.

Web History helps deliver more personalized search results based on the things you've searched for on Google and the sites you've

Web History 1

Web History 2

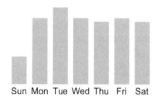

Not sure you are aware of this, but Google keeps a copy of your search history. If you are concerned about privacy, no one has access to your search history but you. To get to your Google Web History, go to : https://accounts.**google**.com/Login?service=hist (as shown on previous page / picture - Web History 1)

Once you are logged in, click the "Account Activity" link in the left sidebar. Once you are on Account Activity, scroll down the page until you reach the "Web History" section. Click that section . Once on the "Web History" page, you will see stats about your search activity on Google. (as shown on previous page / picture - Web History 2)

Scrolling down the page will reveal your most recent searches. (An example is shown below).

Mar 12, 2013

☐	Searched for intitle:Resumé	11:55pm
☐	Searched for Resumé	11:54pm
☐	Searched for (intitle:resume.of OR intitle:resume.by OR intitle:resume.for OR intitle:my.resume OR intitle:"*'s resume") inurl:resume.html (present OR current) (education OR university.of) -template -submit -apply -openings	11:20pm
☐	Searched for (intitle:resume.of OR intitle:resume.by OR intitle:resume.for OR intitle:my.resume OR intitle:"*'s resume") inurl:resume.php (present OR current) (education OR university.of) -template -submit -apply -openings	10:48pm
☐	Searched for (intitle:resume.of OR intitle:resume.by OR intitle:resume.for OR intitle:my.resume OR intitle:"*'s resume") inurl:resume.pdf (present OR current) (education OR university.of) -template -submit -apply -openings	10:46pm
☐	Searched for (intitle:resume.of OR intitle:resume.by OR intitle:resume.for OR intitle:my.resume OR intitle:"*'s resume") inurl:resume (present OR current) (education OR university.of) -template -submit -apply -openings	10:46pm
☐	Searched for (intitle:resume.of OR intitle:resume.by OR intitle:resume.for OR intitle:my.resume OR intitle:"*'s resume") inurl:resume (present OR current) (education OR university.of) -template -submit -apply	10:44pm
☐	Searched for (intitle:resume.of OR intitle:resume.by OR intitle:resume.for OR intitle:"*'s resume") inurl:resume (present OR current) (education OR university.of) -template -submit -apply	10:42pm
☐	Searched for intitle:resume.of | intitle:resume.by | intitle:resume.for | intitle:"*'s resume" inurl:resume.wps (present | current) (education | university.of) -template -submit -apply	10:33pm

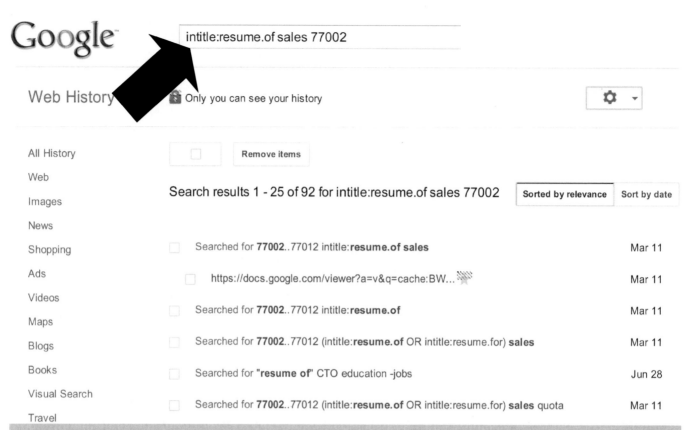

Google

intitle:resume.of sales 77002

Web History   🔒 Only you can see your history   ⚙ ▾

All History	☐ **Remove items**	
Web		
Images	Search results 1 - 25 of 92 for intitle:resume.of sales 77002	**Sorted by relevance** Sort by date
News		
Shopping	☐ Searched for **77002**..77012 intitle:**resume.of sales**	Mar 11
Ads	☐ https://docs.google.com/viewer?a=v&q=cache:BW... 🎇	Mar 11
Videos		
Maps	☐ Searched for **77002**..77012 intitle:**resume.of**	Mar 11
Blogs	☐ Searched for **77002**..77012 (intitle:**resume.of** OR intitle:resume.for) **sales**	Mar 11
Books	☐ Searched for "**resume of**" CTO education -jobs	Jun 28
Visual Search	☐ Searched for **77002**..77012 (intitle:**resume.of** OR intitle:resume.for) **sales** quota	Mar 11
Travel		

At the top of the Web History page is a search box. Simply add keywords and phrases and you will find information of search queries you have done in the past that included those keywords and phrases. You will also see the dates of those searches and the links you clicked on.

How I would use this cool tool:
- Keeping track of old search strings.
- Looking up web pages I clicked on in the past.
- Monitoring how much time I spend on Google.
- If I add to my calendar that I worked on a certain job on a certain day, I can look up the searches I performed on that day and gauge how productive I was with my Google searches. Did I click on a lot of links? Did I do a lot of searches on Google?

Of course, this works well if you search alone. However, I bet most of you reading this, work in groups with other sourcers and recruiters. Am I right? I think I am, which is why I am recommending one of

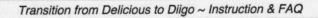

Transition from Delicious to Diigo ~ Instruction & FAQ

Collect and Highlight, Then Remember

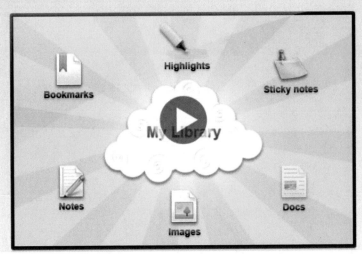

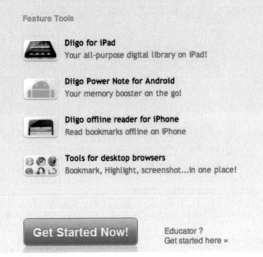

Feature Tools

Diigo for iPad
Your all-purpose digital library on iPad!

Diigo Power Note for Android
Your memory booster on the go!

Diigo offline reader for iPhone
Read bookmarks offline on iPhone

Tools for desktop browsers
Bookmark, Highlight, screenshot...in one place!

Get Started Now!   Educator ?
Get started here »

my all-time favorite tools - **Diigo**. Diigo is a toolbar that lets you bookmark and annotate what you find on the web. (Love 'em! Mean it.) Download the Diigo toolbar now! (www.diigo.com)

Why do I like it so much? Principally for these three reasons:
1. When I find a resume, a LinkedIn profile or a news article that I like, I can bookmark it for later review. I can also annotate it, leave sticky notes on it and highlight parts of it as if it were a real piece of paper.
2. I can keep all of my bookmarks private, public , or make them accessible to a select group of people. This is EXTREMELY useful because it cuts down on recruiters in my group reaching out to the same people. (How would that work? When someone finds a resume online they will see that someone has already bookmarked the resume and move on to source elsewhere. That is, assuming that they are a member of the group I created. As such, we can see each other's notes on resumes, but no one else can. Not even the author of the resume!)
3. I can create a database, bookmark my search strings and refer to them later. (Yay!)There is much more you can do with Diigo beyond what I shared. I highly suggest that you check out their YouTube channel which has a lot of tutorials on it. http://www.youtube.com/diigobuzz

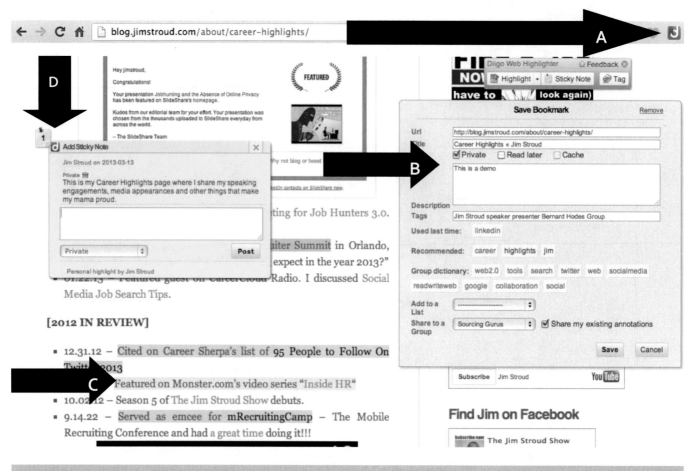

I wanted to give you a glimpse into what its like to work with Diigo.

1. The red ribbon over the Diigo icon (a) lets me know that a bookmark has been made on this page. I see that ribbon because I made the bookmark or, someone in a group I am a member of has made this bookmark or, the bookmark is public and visible to all.
2. By clicking the Diigo icon, I can see the notes that were made in the bookmark (b) and how it was tagged.
3. Using Diigo's highlighter pen (c), I can mark up the parts of the page that I think are most significant.
4. By mousing over the sticky note icon (d), I can see the notation left behind by myself or others.

Alerts

Please enter a valid email address.

Search query: " * is a software engineer at * "

Result type: Everything   ▼

How often: Once a day   ▼

How many: Only the best results   ▼

Your email:

CREATE ALERT   Manage your alerts

Google Alert for today

From: **Google Alerts** <googlealerts-noreply@google.com>

Web   5 new results for " * is a software engineer at * "

Startup uses sensors to find cause of knee pain | Innovation Trail
Tim Cortesi is a software engineer at a Downtown Binghamton company called Sonostics. At the company's offices in Binghamton's startup incubator, he sticks.
innovationtrail.org/.../startup-uses-sensors-find-cause-knee-pai...

SHARE : Blogs : Gen Y: Cross-Generational Q&A Series- Part 5
Brandon Tweed is a Software Engineer at CA Technologies. He was a good candidate for our batch of posts on crisscrossing generations in today's mainframe ...
www.share.org/p/bl/ar/blogaid=226

Personal Finance for Young Professionals | Blog | Jesse Chen
Jesse is a software engineer at Facebook, who

google.com/alerts

I mentioned Google Alerts earlier when I was discussing how to search the news using natural language. I love me some Google Alerts! Why? It lets me put my sourcing on automatic. Back in the day, I would run some web search strings and go through the results later. Unfortunately, Google won't let me save web searches anymore. (sad face) However, I can do a search on everything else: Blogs, News, Video, Discussions and Books.

I suggest setting up your alert notifications for once a week. Otherwise, you may get too many Google Alerts in email to manage efficiently. Umm.. Depending on how many you have set up. I think I used to have 100 or so set up when I could use it to search the web. But hey, that's just me. (Insert smile here)

POWER!

Feeling good about your new found knowledge? You should be! You have learned a lot. Still, there is more you need to do to find those elusive passive candidates.

WOW!

According to InternetWorldStats.com there are a bazillion people on the internet! Okay, **7+ Billion** people to be more exact.

Quite a few of them can be found online using the methods I am sharing in this book. However, a larger segment can be found via creative Employment Branding, Social Networks, New Media and a host of other methods.

Contact me and the good folks over at **Bernard Hodes Group**! We have a lot of training options available to share with you. Among them: Recruiting with **LinkedIn**, Recruiting with **Facebook**, Recruiting with **Google Plus** and Recruiting with **Twitter**. Just FYI...

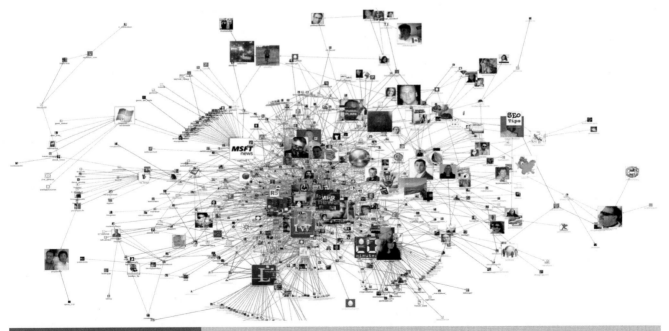

Bernard Hodes Group   www.hodes.com / 888-438-9911 / info@hodes.com

Guess what? You made it to the end of this book. Thanks for sticking it out. As a way of saying thank you for getting this far, I am going to share with you a few more search strings and situations for when I would most likely use them. I hope they prove useful.

I'm not having much luck finding a resume of someone who is an authority in (whatever). So, as a recourse, I look for (whatever) and add emails to my search. Maybe I will get lucky and find someone who is willing to be contacted regarding (whatever) and I can recruit them.

(email.me OR contact.me) ("*@gmail.com" OR "*@hotmail.com" OR "*@yahoo.com" OR "*@outlook.com") **keyword** –intitle:jobs

Hmm... Maybe I should go with actual examples instead of just saying "whatever." Let's see how that works. Okay. Let's say that you are looking for a "Facilities Manager" for an opportunity in the manufacturing industry. And for fun, let's say that this req is an old one and most likely, your org has found all the resumes they are going to find online. (Or, at least they feel that way.) One thing is certain, there are companies out there who hire Facilities Managers. What do they all have in common? Well, one thing for sure, they all have websites. And on said websites, it's a good bet that they have an "About Us" page. Such being the case, I look for company "About Us" pages that have the term "Facilities Manager" posted therein.

Booyah! Here are a couple of examples of what I find: Mauricio Cardoso and Ray Porter.

Tarrant Area Food Bank - **About Us** - Staff
www.tafb.org/staff.html
Risk Management & **Facilities Manager** - Mauricio Cardoso. Allocation Specialist – Linda ... **Warehouse** Manager - Benny Garcia. Logistics & Receiving ...

Staff | **About Us** | CARITAS
www.caritasva.org/**aboutus**_new_staff.html
Ray Porter, **Facilities Manager** (804) 230-1217. James Taylor, Facilities/ ... Michael Gordon, **Warehouse**/Procurement Manager (804) 343-5008. Julie Johnson ...

And here are some search strings I would use to find more of the same.

intitle:about.us (manufacturing | warehouse) "facilities manager"

intitle:about manufacturing "facilities manager" (he | she) -intitle:job

"Facilities Manager" intitle:staff manufacturing -intitle:jobs -submit -apply

"* is the Facilities Manager at * " warehouse

"Facilities Manager" intitle:our.people manufacturing -intitle:jobs -submit -apply

intitle:team "facilities manager * " manufacturing

Now, I will look for some college students with an academic focus on computer science. I will also insure that the results I find are geared towards students graduating in 2013.

" (projected OR expected OR prospective OR estimated) graduation.date * 2013 " education (email OR phone) (intitle:vitae OR intitle:resume) computer.science

I am imagining now that I am looking for some executives who work for a company in the consumer electronics industry. Principally I want a "Vice President of Marketing" but, I am open to other senior management types as well. Here are some search strings I would use to find them. Since they are natural language searches, I try them on Google News as well.

" * joins * as Senior VP" "consumer electronics"
" * promoted to *" "consumer electronics"
" * hires * as Director of" "consumer electronics"
" * named * VP of * " "consumer electronics"
" * approves promotion of * " electronics

" * welcomes * as VP " "consumer electronics"
" * announces * VP of * " "consumer electronics"
" * appoints * VP of * " "consumer electronics""
" * promoted to * of * " "consumer electronics"

As I think about it, I could look for Executives another way as well. How? I could look for articles and blog posts they've written. To do that, I run the following search strings.

about.the.writer " * is the (CEO OR founder OR VP)" "consumer electronics"

intitle:about.the.author " * is vice president of " "consumer electronics"

"about the author" " * is vice president of " "consumer electronics"

Let me switch gears a bit and give you something else to consider when sourcing. Every industry has a newsletter, magazine or some sort of publication associated with it. If you can find such a resource relevant to the industry you are looking for, you might find some leads. After all, featured in the articles of those publications are quotes from people in the field and/or an interview of some kind. Get me? Here are a few search strings for tracking down engineers who work in... umm... Sanitation.

intitle:sanitation (intitle:magazine | intitle:quarterly | intitle:journal | intitle:news | intitle:newsletter) " * an engineer "

intitle:report water.and.sanitation " (he OR she) is an engineer"

inurl:news ~sanitation " (he OR she) is an engineer"

Now, on to something different. Earlier in the book, I gave a list of suggestions on how to compile a list of competitor (and related) companies to target with your searches. I want to suggest one more strategy. Consider recruiting out of companies being heralded as producers of award-winning products. Who knows? You might discover an innovative startup with talent ripe for the picking. Here are a few search strings for finding innovative companies in Cloud Computing.

intitle:award.winning niche "cloud computing"

intitle:best.of "cloud computing" (award OR honored OR won)

(intitle:award.winning OR intitle:nominated.for OR intitle:best.of.breed) "cloud computing"

If you like this strategy, a few more words you might want to play with in your searches are: "Top 100," "Best Companies" and "Fastest Growing."

Umm... I am beginning to feel like I am rambling, so let me close out with two more tactics that can prove useful to you.

There are several websites available that allow users to store documents online for free. For example, Google has "Google Drive" (formerly "Google Docs") which lets people upload all kinds of content to a virtual drive. Most of the things people upload is for their private use. However, there are quite a few pieces of content out there made available to the public. Among them, resumes. Check out what I see when I site search **Google Docs.**

 site:docs.google.com intitle:resume present education "software engineer"

Web   Images   Maps   Shopping   More ▾   Search tools

About 14,600 results (0.29 seconds)

Chris Camp **Resume** - Brooklyn, NY - Google Drive
https://docs.google.com/document/d/.../edit
SOFTWARE ENGINEER, SRA International, INC. New York, NY June 2005 – **Present**.
A National Company specializing in providing consulting and web-based ...

Resume - Google Drive - Google Docs
https://docs.google.com/document/d/.../edit
May 2012 - **present**: Senior **Software Engineer**, Tidemark.net. Implemented features in calculation engine (Java, Spring); Implemented high availability test suite ...

Resume - Mark St. John - Google Drive
https://docs.google.com/document/d/1qD9VFVQwMcmaw.../edit
EXPERIENCE. Senior **Software Engineer**, Google. Chicago, Illinois — 2012-**Present**.
Google Affiliate Network frontend and backend **software engineer**.

Current resume - Google Drive
https://docs.google.com/document/d/...Mld2tfbLgfLBZ5o/edit
July 2012-**Present** ... Software Engineer - Android ... Senior **Software Engineer** ...
Introduced **current** software practices to the project, including Subversion ....
Education. 1983-1988. The Ohio State University, Columbus, OH. Major in computer ...

Below are search strings for finding Software Engineer resumes on sites where users can upload documents and make them available to the public (for free, by the way.)

site:scribd.com intitle:resume present education "software engineer"

site:docstoc.com intitle:resume (education | university.of) software.engineer -sample -template

site:slideshare.net intitle:resume (education | university.of) software.engineer -sample -template

You might be wondering how I target such sites like "docstoc.com" (above) and mine it for resumes. Well, it's a simple formula. So simple that I perform it subconsciously.

- I scan the search results to see which URLs appear more than once.
- I site search to see if Google has indexed a large number of the site's pages.
- I visit the site where the leads are coming from.
- I look for words or phrases that would most likely appear on all (or most) pages on that website.
- I create searches based on webpage commonalities and begin mining for leads.

Hmm… let me do a real life example to bring this point home even further. Let's say I am still looking for a Software Engineer. Among the results, I see the following:

Thierry Bodhuin's Public Profile
www.plaxo.com/profile/showPublic/bodhuin
Researcher - Software Engineer - University of Sannio - RCOST - Research...
Thierry Bodhuin's Public Profile on Plaxo. ... Thierry Bodhuin 17 connections.
Researcher - Software Engineer, University of Sannio - RCOST - Research.

The first thing I notice is the title. It has the words "Public Profile" in it and someone's name. More than likely all of their profile pages are set up that way. I also see the words "profile" and "showPublic" are in the URL. Finally, I see that the result is from plaxo.com. I wonder how many pages Google has in its database from Plaxo.com?

Google site:plaxo.com

Web	Images	Maps	Shopping	More ▾	Search tools

About 9,280,000 results (0.27 seconds)

Google promotion

Try Google Webmaster Tools
www.google.com/webmasters/
Do you own **plaxo.com**? Get indexing and ranking data from Google.

Plaxo - your address book for life.
www.plaxo.com/
The leading smart address book, Plaxo unifies your contacts across sources,
proactively updates contact info, and syncs your complete address book with the ...
3,014 people +1'd this

Plaxo Customer Community
forum.plaxo.com/
Feb 15, 2008 – 45 people asked this! Click Mini_star-
b473cd3271224a01bebf1279a57d57a4 to add your vote! * 45. De-Duper is ineffective ·
mredshaw2 ...

Plaxo for Business - Volume Licenses - Volume Sales | Plaxo
www.plaxo.com/business

Hmm... Google says that they have 9+ million of Plaxo's webpages indexed. Good to know. Why? Since so much is stored, I am confident I will find something when I look. But first, let me gather a bit more intel by visiting the profile I found initially.

Oh! Before I continue, let me give you a heads up on something. Should you ever see in your results words like: "pages," "members," "profile," "home," "homepage" or "my," then chances are that website is a good candidate for being mined for leads the way I am demonstrating now with Plaxo. Just FYI...

Okay, I digress.

 plaxo | Power to the address book

👍 Like 🄵 41,104 people like this. Sign Up to see what your friends like.

ℊ +1

b

Thierry Bodhuin 17 connections

Researcher - Software Engineer, University of Sannio - RCOST - Research...

Benevento

Fu

a

Me on the Web

'You'	bodhuin
	bodhuin
	bodhuin.dyndns.org

c

Professional Summary

Software Architect Consultant, Development Processes, Software Engineer & Researcher at University of Sannio, Italy

d

Work/Education

Work Experience **e**

University of Sannio - RCOST - Research Centre On Software Technology / **Researcher - Software Engineer**
2003 - Present

Once on Mr. Bodhuin's profile, I look for things that might be on other Plaxo profiles. Things like the (a) "Me on the Web" module in the sidebar, (b) how many connections he has, how sections of the profile are named. For example (c) "Professional Summary," (d) "Work/Education," (e) "Work Experience" and further down the page (not shown above) "Education" and "Public Stream."

Armed with that data, I begin experimenting with search strings to see which give me the most and/or best results. Just for the sake of your curiosity, here are some of the searches I performed and the results.

site:plaxo.com intitle:public.profile [14.500 results]

site:plaxo.com "software engineer" [42,400 results]

site:plaxo.com inurl:profile "software engineer" [13,500 results]

site:plaxo.com inurl:profile "Work/Education" "software engineer" [8 results]

site:plaxo.com "Work Experience" "software engineer" [14 results]

site:plaxo.com intitle:public.profile "software engineer" [180 results]

site:plaxo.com "public stream" "software engineer" [8 results]

I noticed that the larger the search results , the more likely I was going to come across pages I did not want to see. Namely, jobs and career advice, etc. This is why its important to experiment ! You have to tweak, tweak, tweak to get all the data you can. Make sense? Hope so...

Although I have more I can show you, this feels like a good place to stop. Battling my inner search geek is not an easy thing. (wink)

Please do keep **Bernard Hodes Group** (www.hodes.com) in mind should your recruiting organization ever need training in Sourcing and/or Social Recruiting. I promise you that this book has only scratched the surface. (Operators are standing by.)

So, until then, happy hunting!

Jim Stroud

THE END **Get on my mailing list! Go to: jimstroud.com/rf**

Okay, so if you are reading this, you may be thinking , "Jim, I thought the book was over."
To which I would reply, "It is... kinda."

You ever watch a movie and at the end, when the credits are rolling, they sneak in a bit more of the movie before its really over? Well, this is like that. I am writing to slide in a couple of more things before you flip to the final (really, really final) page.

RELATED SEARCHES UPDATE

Back on page **57,** I showed you how to refine your search by "related search." Well, on a whim, I returned to that page to perform another search and guess what? It was no longer there! I think it might have been a glitch or something. Still, I felt compelled to mention it. I am more than confident that Google will return that related search function. Why? Google has always had it in one way or another. A section of related searches was once a fixture at the bottom of all web searches. Prior to that, Google had something called the "Wonder Wheel" for doing related searches. (I miss that thing.) Before that... Well, I think you get me. Related searches may be gone today, but look for them to return tomorrow.

AROUND

Hmm... What else? Oh! On pages **28 - 39,** I discuss Google Search Operators. Well, I sort of, kind of, forgot to mention one. So, here it is - "AROUND." With the "AROUND" command you can search for text that's nearby a keyword you are searching for. For example, let's say that you want Google to find the phrase "is a software engineer" within 9 words of the phrase "cloud computing." This is how you would do that.

"is a software engineer" AROUND(9) "cloud computing"

Notice how "AROUND" is in all caps? Also, see how the number "9" is in parenthesis? You have to type the search exactly as I have for it to work. Just fyi... Feel free to adjust the AROUND number higher or lower. By doing so, you will get more or fewer search results. Make sense?

I have noticed that AROUND is **not** perfect in that, some search results show terms that are not in exact proximity as I requested. In other words, if I look for a certain word to be mentioned within 5 words of another, they are sometimes found within 6 or more words. It all comes down to what's out there online and how closely Google can find a result that best matches what I'm looking for.

" is a software engineer" AROUND(9) "cloud computing"

About Infomercial.TV, Inc.
www.infomercial.tv/about.html

August Kleimo **is a software engineer with expertise in cloud** computing, web-based tools, complex data-driven web sites, and data mining solutions. Prior to ...

Turn a Business Idea into a Validated Business Model in 8 Weeks
www.startathlon.com/

Nick Boucart **is a software engineer, a web and cloud** computing guru, works a lot with startups as a Sirris adviser. He is one of the co-authors of the 'The Art of ...

Taking Linux Filesystems to the Space Age: Space Maps in Ext4 ...
www.linuxplumbersconf.org/2010/ocw/proposals/43

Shweta Jain **is a software engineer with experience in the cloud** computing, storage and Linux kernel domains. She has worked on enhancing the features of ...

Here are a few more searches using the AROUND search operator, just to get your imagination going.

```
"my current position" AROUND(7) "software engineer"  ext:doc
"I managed a team" AROUND(9) "software engineers" site:net
intitle:resume  "computer science" AROUND(4) "graduation date * 2013"
inurl:(resume OR vitae) "school of life sciences" AROUND(4) 2010..2013
intitle:profile "my work ethic" AROUND(11) sales
```

Okay, I think I am **now** at the very end. One way to know for sure! Of course, turn the page.

Sourcing is cool.

Made in the USA
Columbia, SC
12 July 2017